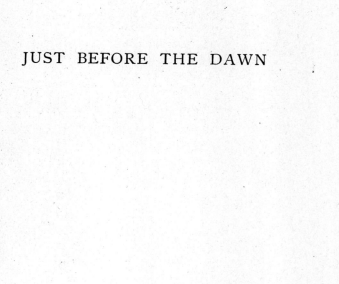

JUST BEFORE THE DAWN

THE MACMILLAN COMPANY
NEW YORK · BOSTON · CHICAGO
DALLAS · SAN FRANCISCO

MACMILLAN & CO., LIMITED
LONDON · BOMBAY · CALCUTTA
MELBOURNE

THE MACMILLAN CO. OF CANADA, LTD.
TORONTO

NINOMIYA SONTOKU, THE SAGE.

(*Frontispiece*)

JUST BEFORE THE DAWN

THE LIFE AND WORK OF

NINOMIYA SONTOKU

BY

ROBERT CORNELL ARMSTRONG, M.A.

KOBE, JAPAN

This book describes the conditions in Japan just before the dawn of the Meiji Era, the age of enlightenment. The awakening that took place in Japan has since been spreading over the whole East.

New York

THE MACMILLAN COMPANY

1912

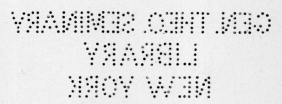
Norwood Press
J. S. Cushing Co. — Berwick & Smith Co.
Norwood, Mass., U.S.A.

TO THE MEMORY OF

MY MOTHER

SOPHRONIA CORNELL ARMSTRONG

FOREWORD

THE work here presented to the public is, in my estimation, one of the most important hitherto coming from the field of Canadian Missions. Christian Missions in Japan, China, and India have to deal with problems very different from those presented in Missions to the native tribes of our own country or of Africa. These nations have an intellectual, moral, and religious history which cannot be ignored by those engaged in the work of Christian Missions among them. The more thoroughly we understand their moral and intellectual attitude, character, and ideas, and sympathize with their needs as well as appreciate that which they hold of truth, the more likely are we to do them good and to help them to more excellent things.

But the utility of such studies, as are here presented, is not confined to the missionary and his work. The scientific student who is interested in the study of man, especially in his moral and religious development, will find most important material for his purpose in this work of Mr. Armstrong. Here we have almost within our own times one of those moral movements which have at various times so profoundly influenced the human race. Perhaps some day we may have a comparative study of such movements, embracing various races and civilizations, but this will only be possible when the separate materials have been collected for the use of the scientific student and, as here, brought within his reach.

A characteristic of this particular movement, and one which marks it in common with other similar movements in the East, is its practical character. In this respect it resembles the work of Confucius. He grappled with the task of government and obedience to law, the Farmer Sage with that of economics and simple, yet sufficient, and healthful life ; the older Mosaic system touched both. Both laid good foundations for a higher spiritual life, which is always more permanent when built upon a simple, yet sufficient, temporal life.

But to the ordinary Canadian reader this book will also have its interest. It will give us a better understanding of a people who will always be near neighbors, and who must influence our future history under the higher law and mission of commerce. It will serve to remove many misapprehensions and give us a fellow-feeling for those who have the same wants and perplexities and sins in their human life as have we ourselves.

N. BURWASH.

VICTORIA COLLEGE,
November 7, 1911.

CONTENTS

INTRODUCTION

OUTLINE OF EARLY REFORMS AND ETHICAL THOUGHT IN JAPAN

PART I

THE LIFE OF NINOMIYA SONTOKU

CONTENTS

PART II

THE TEACHINGS OF NINOMIYA SONTOKU

PART III

AN ESTIMATE OF HIS TEACHINGS

LIST OF ILLUSTRATIONS

GUIDE TO JAPANESE PRONUNCIATION

a *like* a *in* father   ai *as in* aisle

e *like* e *in* hen   ei *as in* weigh

i *like* i *in* sin   au ⎫
               as o *in* bone

o *like* o *in* bone   ō ⎭

u *like* oo *in* boot   ū *as* oo *in* soon

Consonants as in English.

G is always hard, but sometimes it has the nasal ng.

Z *before* u = dz.

Double consonants are both sounded; *e.g.* Nik-ko is not Niko.

INTRODUCTION

RACIAL prejudice has played a great rôle in the history of the world. Under certain conditions this has been of great value in leading men, with an utter contempt for their opponents, to attempt and actually achieve what would otherwise have been impossible. Under other conditions, however, it may lead, and actually has led, to the greatest injustice and cruelty. In many ways it may be shown that this extreme prejudice is being rapidly changed in our day. The rapid development of commercial relations between the most remote parts of the world has led to an exchange of products, and the relations thus set up between buyers and sellers have compelled men of the most diverse races to try to understand one another, so far, at least, as financial interests are concerned. The profit and loss account has led men to overcome strong racial and other prejudices, and has made those of widely different character and religion unite in the effort to obtain wealth.

The work of Christian missionaries has been hampered by racial prejudices on both sides. It has, however, now become recognized as of the most vital concern that those who would teach should profoundly understand the attitude of those to whom they would bring their message. In our day this racial aloofness is breaking down before the evident fact that beneath the differences of men there are great fundamental relations with which the color of the skin, the build of the body, or even social customs have no vital concern. Works written *about* other races show this, but nothing can make it as clear to the ordinary man as the simple statement of the people themselves. Every one recognizes that a mother's love is so bound up in her little one that any mother forced to give up her baby boy, as was Ninomiya's mother because of her poverty, would like her be heart-broken, and like her, too, would welcome any help which would enable her to have her own. Here the mothers of Christendom stand on a plane with those of China, India, or Japan. So, too, do we praise the affection displayed by fourteen-year-old Ninomiya in coming to the help of his mother in her trouble. These things are not peculiarly Japanese, but are of equal value the world over.

It is not, however, so evident that economically, morally, religiously, the same deep-seated struggle is met wherever men who have an organized society or worship are found; in fact, one often meets the statement that in these relations each race is a unit, differing so essentially from others that it is foolish to try to introduce an economic theory, a moral life, or a religious system to a foreign race, no matter how satisfactory it has been found among other peoples. The "Life and Work of Ninomiya Sontoku" may do more to dispel this illusion than many works written from a profound philosophic basis. It is practice as opposed to theory. Ninomiya may prove at once that economically and morally, at least, exactly the same problems have been met in Japan that would be met under similar conditions among any other people.

The cultivation of the land in Japan was found by Ninomiya to be at the basis of their economic success. The great difficulty in the way of such cultivation was the moral indifference of the people, manifested in the same desire to get something without paying for it, to conquer nature without sweating, that one may find in America or Europe or elsewhere; and the immorality which he met is exactly the same kind of immorality which hinders progress everywhere. In an absolutely fundamental sense the oneness of the Japanese with the races of Christendom in their economic struggle and their moral problems is seen at once in the work which lies before us. No more valuable contribution to the understanding of the Japanese in a sympathetic, helpful way is possible than in the presentation of such lives as those of Ninomiya and others who, like him, have helped to make modern Japan.

The question of the religious solidarity of the race is not seriously touched by Ninomiya; his great aim was economic rather than religious; even morality seems to have been to him a means to an economic end rather than a thing in itself. But if men are one in their economic and social problems, why need we suppose that they differ so widely religiously? The only excuse for such a view is that religion is too often confused with the theories which men hold of a theological nature about the great fundamental religious facts. If men have religious needs which are more or less met by each of the great religious systems of the world, it is no proof that these needs are different in races which have, for many reasons, adopted one form of solution rather than another. That a man's life is profoundly influenced by what he thinks of other men is surely quite evident entirely apart from any injunction to "love one's neighbor as one's self," or "to do unto another as we would have him do to us"; and the fact that in life we are always face to face with conditions over which our likes and dislikes — our wills — have no control, except by absolutely following what we commonly call law, is so clear that no discussion of it is necessary. What if one race

call it fate, another the reign of law, or others
the Will of God, the fact remains that the condition is recognized by all. The theory of the condition, however, differs. If the Christian nations
of the world have found in the teaching of Jesus
of Nazareth a solution for the deepest of life's
problems which they believe to be more satisfactory than all others, they have exactly the same
right to present that solution to the races of the
world that they have to carry to them the story
of their successes in astronomy, in physical science,
or in government. The day is far past when it is
possible to look upon men as widely different in
the fundamental conditions of life. The day is also
surely passing when Christians will want to go
to foreign peoples with a religion backed up by
any authority save that of its ability to meet the
deepest needs of men.

Considered from this point of view, the study
of Ninomiya may well prove a real missionary
stimulus to Christians, if only their faith in their
religion be that of the man who, having tried it
himself, is willing to recommend it to others. Mr.
Armstrong's work is so marked by his evident
sympathy with the struggles of the Japanese that
one need hardly say that in the work before us
an absolutely faithful picture has been given of
that part of Japan covered by the work of Ninomiya. It is not the Japan of to-day, and yet

no one can thoughtfully peruse this work without
being convinced that the only difference between
the Japan of Ninomiya, the Japan of to-day, and
the other nations of the world is found in inci-
dental externals; in the deep needs of life we are
one.

ALBERT H. ABBOTT.

UNIVERSITY OF TORONTO,
July, 1912.

AUTHOR'S PREFACE

AFTER the Russo-Japanese War the teachings of Ninomiya Sontoku became suddenly popular. The Home Department of the Japanese Government, acting in coöperation with the Educational Department, endeavored to introduce them into the whole school system of Japan. One result of this propaganda was that the magazines and papers of Japan issued many articles on the life and teachings of Ninomiya. His teachings emphasize a high ideal of life, with careful and economical methods of utilizing the resources of the country. They are, therefore, particularly in place in Japan at the present time, on account of the war debt which has to be met.

In my work in Japan I spent five years in Hamamatsu in Totomi Province, which is one of the strongholds of the "Hotoku" Society. There I met some of its members, and soon realized that it was essential to my work that I should know, in an intimate way and through personal investigation, what they believed. Failing to find any adequate account of their doctrines in English, Mr. K. Kanazawa, an intimate friend, consented to translate from Japanese records a short account of Ninomiya's work.

What I thus learned increased my interest both in the man and his teachings, and with the assistance of the Rev. T. Ota of Kanazawa City, I was enabled to gather most of the anecdotes and teachings found in this work, which one will easily realize as he reads are, for the most part, nothing more than translations.

In putting these teachings into English I have aimed, not so much at expressing them in literary form, as at giving a faithful picture of this attempt of the Japanese to solve in an earnest, thoughtful way their economic, moral, and religious problems. I have attempted to bring out, wherever possible, the common human side of Japanese character, and hope that what is here presented may at least help to give those who read it a broader sympathy for that wonderful people.

Mr. Tomeoka, who, though a Christian, is an ardent follower of Ninomiya, not only gave me the privilege of using his books, but drew my attention to others which I had not seen. He said in a letter to me: " Ninomiya Sontoku is one of the best men among Japanese. If you introduce his work and character to Europeans it will be the demand of the age."

I am greatly indebted to Dr. A. H. Abbott and Professor James Mavor, of the University of

Toronto; Dr. N. Burwash, of Victoria University; Mr. Galen M. Fisher, of the Y. M. C. A., Tokyo; Dr. G. W. Knox, of Union Seminary, New York; and to Dr. and Mrs. F. C. Stephenson, of the Forward Movement for Missions, for their suggestions in the publication of this work.

I leave myself open to criticism in the Introduction for attempting to outline Japanese religious thought so briefly, but I justify myself in doing so because, absurd as it may seem, there are so many Westerners who not only know nothing about the subject, but even imagine that the Japanese have had no valuable civilization until they came in touch with the West about a half century ago. Even my brief summary of their ideas may lead men to see what elements of a religious, moral, and economic nature surrounded Japanese boys as influences in producing such strong character and manhood as found in the Farmer Sage.

JUST BEFORE THE DAWN

CHAPTER I

" BEGINNINGS "

"THESE Japanese are supremely curious,[1] eager to be instructed to the highest degree. . . . Their curiosity is such that they become importunate; they ask questions and argue without knowing how to make an end of it; eager to have an answer and to communicate what they have learned to others. . . . I wrote to Father Rodriguez and, in his absence, to the Rector of the College of Coimbra, to send to the [Japanese] Universities none but men tried and approved by your holy charity. They will be much more persecuted than they believe; at all hours of the day and a part of the night they will be importuned by visits and questions. . . . They will have no time either to pray or for meditation, or to collect themselves, at the beginning especially, no time to say a daily mass; replying to questions will occupy them so much that they will scarcely find time to recite the office;

[1] Cf. "A History of Japan," by James Murdock, M.A., Vol. I, page 5.

to eat or to sleep." So wrote Francis Xavier in 1551 A.D., and the picture of the Japanese which he here gives may well be taken as descriptive of them in all ages. In more ways than one they resemble the ancient Greeks,[1] who spent their time telling and learning some new thing. Centuries of moral, religious, and intellectual culture precede their modern achievements. It is folly for certain Western writers to claim that the progress of Modern Japan is essentially due to imitation, or to the external artificial influences of Western civilization.

Professor Anesaki-Masahar,[2] of the Imperial University, Tokyo, in a short Religious History of Japan revised for private circulation from an article written for the Encyclopædia Americana, divides the Religious History of Japan into five periods.

First, "The Prehistoric Religion," which was an unorganized native worship not unlike early Greek mythology. Near the end of this period (circa 300 A.D.) Chinese learning and Confucianism were first introduced into Japan from Korea.

Second, "The First Period of Buddhism" in the sixth century A.D. was followed by seven centuries of steady development, during which various teachings of Buddhism from China were introduced.

[1] Acts 17 : 21.
[2] Professor of the Science of Religion and Kahn Scholar for 1907–1908.

Third, "Religious Struggles," which continued for three hundred years, beginning with the thirteenth century when more original, and more distinctively Japanese sects of Buddhism were founded. This era was one of political as well as religious struggle.

Fourth, "Peace and Slumber" — caused by the supremacy of the Tokugawa Shogunate,[1] which continued from circa 1600 to 1868 A.D. During this period Modern Confucianism was introduced and developed; the National Shinto religion revised and Buddhism declined in power.

Fifth, "The New Era — Reawakening and Fermentation." In this period Christianity is introduced, Buddhism is being revised and purified, and the religious condition of the people is very unsettled. It is a transition period. Ninomiya Sontoku, with whose life and teachings the present work is particularly concerned, lived at the end of the fourth period. He was more or less influenced by all the ethical and religious thought of Japan up to his time as well as by the economic and moral conditions of his own age. An introduction to the exposition of his life and teachings must deal with the more important of these elements.

In the prehistoric age (600 B.C. to circa 300 A.D.) a primitive spirit-worship which afterward de-

[1] Military rule.

veloped as Shintoism represented the religious superstitions of the people. There were gods and goddesses, and everything that was regarded as mysterious or powerful in the heavens, the air, nature and man, was made an object of worship.

About 284 A.D.[1] Confucianism was first introduced from Korea, and from the introduction of Buddhism until about 1600 it was not thought to be out of harmony with Buddhism. It taught practical morality and played a great part in making the laws which were to govern the people. It taught the five relations, with their corresponding virtues: (1) Ruler and subject — loyalty; (2) Father and son — filial piety; (3) Husband and wife — separateness, *i.e.* the performance of their separate duties; (4) Elder and younger brother — affection; (5) Friends — faithfulness.

In addition to these, there were the five cardinal virtues: benevolence, righteousness, propriety, wisdom, and sincerity. This ethical code was based on a belief in Heaven which was thought of as supporting its followers, conferring blessing on the good and punishment on the evil, sustaining true men and protecting the truth. The introduction of Buddhism, which soon gained supremacy and, to a

[1] Cf. Transactions of the Asiatic Society of Japan, Vol. XXXIV, Part IV. Article by Professor A. Lloyd, of the Imperial University. Korean records make this date 384 A.D.

4

large extent, absorbed the distinctive influence of Confucianism, prevented it from developing into much more than a formal discussion of words and phrases.

CHAPTER II

" BUDDHISM IN OUTLINE "

BUDDHISM was first introduced in the thirteenth
year of the Emperor Kim-mei, 552 A.D.,[1] and for
several centuries had a dominating influence on
Japanese social and political life. It first came
to Japan from Korea, but was soon followed by
importations from China. It is not necessary to
even mention the various sects of Buddhism in
this introduction; but in a general way Buddhism
was divided into two great schools, known as the
Southern and Northern. The former was a religious system, without a personal God, creator, or
ruler of the universe. Man was composed of
five elements, which separated at death to come
together in some new combination which was influenced by the merit or demerit[2] of the former
being, thus seeming to imply, though really denying, the identity of the two, in anything like a

[1] Cf. "A Short History of Twelve Buddhist Sects," translated
from original Japanese by Bunyiu Nanjio, M.A., Oxford; Lecturer
of Sanscrit in the Imperial University.

[2] Kharma.

soul. Thus the law of retribution affected the new being, who suffered or was rewarded for the deeds done in the former existence. A story told me by a Buddhist priest in Japan will illustrate this great law, although to-day no intelligent Japanese can believe it literally. A certain priest far famed for his virtue was summoned to assist his ruler in a ceremony celebrating some notable event in his dominions. On the appointed day the priest arrived at the palace. The king was playing chess with one of his subjects, and was so absorbed in his game that he cried out, "Cut off !" (Japanese for " Checkmate ") just as the attendant entered to announce the priest. The attendant, thinking that his master meant him to execute the priest, seized him and cut off his head. When the king heard of it, he had the attendant's head cut off. Commenting on this, the Buddhist teacher explained that those events illustrated the law of retribution. This tragedy was long destined to be transacted because in a former existence when the priest was a farmer, he had killed a frog, which was the form in which the king was supposed to exist at that time. Human existence, birth, and death were evils caused by desire, which it was the aim of every Buddhist to extinguish, and thus escape existence and enter Nirvana, thus ceasing to be an individual.

According to this Southern School "the virtuous man abstained from women, royal palaces,[1] beautiful things, and riches."

The Northern School, sometimes called pantheistic, sometimes theistic, Buddhism, is alone found in Japan. It has had great influence. According to Northern, or Mahayana, Buddhism,[2] he who would be truly virtuous must extol the spirit of wisdom, the love of virtue, the life of retirement, and practise patience and firmness. Buddha[3] is acknowledged at once a transcendent and immanent being, the soul of all living beings, whose attributes are eternal manifestations of power. The eternity of his being is seen, in that all things are one in him, who is not only manifested in nature but especially in the "Incarnate One," in whom are stored infinite possibilities. He has all power to produce good; he is the great essence of the visible and invisible worlds; all different forms of the universe are but different manifestations of him who is unchangeable and indestructible; he is the One Mind eternal and full of purity.

In Northern Buddhism there are two great divisions based on the method of attaining Buddha-

[1] Transactions of the Asiatic Society of Japan, Vol. XXII, Part III, from page 343. An article by Professor A. Lloyd.

[2] *Ibid.*, Vol. XXII, Part III, page 343.

[3] Cf. "Awakening of Faith," by Ashvagosha.

hood. The older division teaches that one must
enter Nirvana by one's own power, by the help of
many rules and precepts, and by obeying the five
prohibitions, which forbid the taking of life,[1]
stealing, lying, adultery, and intoxication. A man
may by steady perseverance through several stages
of rebirth finally attain Buddhahood. In this
connection, when a child resembles any of his
ancestry, the ancestor is thought to be renewing
his relation with the material world, and by natural
growth forcing matter into the same shape that it
had in its former existence, just as the seed forces
the nourishment it receives from the air and soil,
into the same shaped plant from which it fell.[2]
Before attaining Buddhahood, a man must pass
through the five lower worlds; viz., the world of
sensuous desire and contact with gross matter;
the world of form, where matter is refined and
becomes spiritual; the world of intelligence,[3] where
existence cannot be sensed, but is known only to
thought. After this he may enter Nirvana, where
existence ceases, and essence alone remains.

[1] Not that life is sacred, but because it involves suffering. The
great virtue of Buddhism is Mercy.

[2] Ninomiya refers to this; the name for this process in Japanese
is "Inkwa," "In" meaning seed, and "kwa," flower. Cf. also
Ingersoll Lecture, 1908, by William S. Bigelow, on "Buddhism
and Immortality," page 52.

[3] Cf. Transactions of the Asiatic Society of Japan, Vol.
XXII, Part III, Chap. IV, page 369.

Nirvana is at once the most important and the most difficult doctrine of Buddhism. Its importance lies in the fact that it is the goal of all Buddhistic aspiration. Its difficulty, for most Westerners at least, lies chiefly in the fact that it tries to picture the unthinkable. The idea does not originate with Buddha, but goes back into the older ideas of Indian thought. The word originally meant "The state of a blown-out flame," [1] so that the prime meaning of the doctrine centres around the extinction of the fires of desire, especially the desire for individual existence. When Buddha sat under the Bo tree, he attained this enlightenment. When he died over forty years later, he sank into the "Great Birthless," from which there is no desire to be reborn; viz. Nirvana.

One who has reached this sublime self-renunciation may sink back into the limitless sea of consciousness from which he has come and from which the desire for individual existence has separated him during ages of transmigration. Nirvana has been called an unchangeable state of conscious

[1] For further reference see the following: (1) Cf. Transactions of Asiatic Society of Japan, Vol. XXII, Part III, Chapter IV, page 369. (2) Ingersoll Lectures for 1908, " Buddhism and Immortality," by William S. Bigelow, M.D. (3) "Sacred Books of the East." " Life of Buddha," by Ashvagosha. Rys Davids Jataka. (4) " Buddhism in its Connection with Brahminism and Hinduism," by Sir Monier-Monier Williams.

blessedness, completely cut off from any recollection of all former states of existence. To most modern psychologists, this means practical, individual annihilation.

There is ultimately but one consciousness which is continuous. Therefore all beings are essentially one. If one strike another, he really strikes himself, for sometime the injury will return to him; [1] so if one benefit another, the benefit will return. The difference between the various beings and worlds lies in the amount of this universal consciousness they possess; an animal has less than a man, and a man less than a saint. But it lies in his power to obtain more, or to lose some of what he already possesses. If one is very lustful and self-centred, he will be reborn an animal. If he is very generous and altruistic, he will be reborn in one of the higher worlds. If he is foolish enough to cling to existence and encourage selfish desire, he will pay for it by getting more of the lower world. As the Hindu writer expressed it, "What will you have?" quoth God. "Take it and pay for it." If one follow the well-known Buddhist maxim, "Abstain from evil, practise the good, [2] cleanse the heart," he will after long ages enter Nirvana.

[1] By the law of retribution.
[2] Cf. Transactions of the Asiatic Society, Vol. XXII, Part III, page 366.

According to the older schools of Buddhism which emphasized salvation by one's own power, literally self-power, a man might help himself to suppress his feelings and desires by practising various methods of meditation. (1) There [1] was "The Breath-Counting Contemplation," in which a man sat in a quiet place and counted the number of times he inhaled and exhaled the air; (2) "The Impurity Contemplation," in which a man recalls the foulness of the body in order to crush out sexual inclination; (3) "The Moon-Disk Contemplation," in which the worshipper gazes intently at a bright disk of the full moon hanging in front of his breast, in order that the brightness which at first merely strikes its surface may penetrate the breast [2] and flood the mind with light, thus taking away any foreign elements that belong to the unenlightened; (4) "The Water-Concept Contemplation," by which one must dwell on the thought of his body melting into water until it actually seems to do so. A story is told of Esshin Sozu,[3] a famous Japanese priest, practising the water-conception contemplation in the presence of a guest until the guest, becoming nervous, struck him with a

[1] Cf. Transactions of the Asiatic Society of Japan, Vol. XXXVIII, Part II, page 29.

[2] Literally, heart.

[3] This is found in a Japanese book called "Koso Jitsu Den Bukkyo-Kaku Shu."

cushion and brought him suddenly out of it. A
few days later Esshin, meeting him, complained
that he thought the cushion still remained in his
shoulder, as he still felt the pain caused by the
stroke. He did not recover until he had again lost
himself in this "Water Contemplation" and his
friend had gone through the form of pulling out
the cushion. The story is of interest because it
resembles very much the methods of modern hyp-
notism.

In the third period of Japanese history, mentioned by Professor Anesaki, the older Buddhist
sects, which taught salvation by one's own power,
were losing their influence, and the longing of the
people led to the rise of a new and almost
distinctively[1] Japanese form of Buddhism. This
form emphasized salvation by faith in another ;
namely, Amida, the redeemer of measureless light,
who dwelt in the "Western-pure-land."[2] By this
faith, all beings, no matter how sinful, might attain
to the perfection of Buddha by faith in Amida's
Vow[3] to save all who sincerely call upon him and
may thus reach paradise, escaping the tortures of

[1] There were several great teachers responsible for these de-
velopments, three Indian, four Chinese, and three Japanese, so
that this teaching did not originate entirely in Japan.

[2] "Jodo," paradise.

[3] Cf. Transactions of the Asiatic Society of Japan, Vol. XVII,
Part I, "The Gobunsho," by Mr. James Troop.

hell, over which the law [1] of retribution reigns. It allowed its priests to marry, and thus made the home the centre of religious life. In this "True Buddhism," we see a reaction from the austerities and supermundane character of the older teaching, and also from transmigration and what seems to be practical individual annihilation. According to this new Buddhism, a man need not retire to a hermit's cave in order to lead a holy life; faith in the one supreme Buddha will save him, even if he is not a worshipper of all the other Buddhas. Japanese Buddhism has in this sect a superficial resemblance to Christianity. This resemblance is counteracted by the older Buddhist conception of existence and life to which it is attached. If existence is evil, and faith in Amida will transport one to paradise, then the logical result of the union of two such doctrines is suicide. A story is told that several women whose husbands had been killed in war, after hearing the doctrine from Honen Shonin, deliberately walked into the sea and drowned themselves, to escape from their wretched existence.

Professor Lloyd, of the Imperial University, Tokyo, Japan, is trying to trace some historical connection between this form of Buddhism and

[1] Transactions of the Asiatic Society of Japan, Vol. XIV, Part I, page 8, note 13.

Christianity. Whether that be possible or not, this new Buddhism should give the Westerner a point of contact that, if taken advantage of, should some day lead the Japanese to recognize Christ as the historical "Amida, Lord of measureless light and life," whose teachings are based on an optimistic view of the universe and existence, which may be said to centre around the ideas contained in the Fatherhood of God and in eternal life. It was Christ's mission to reveal these.

CHAPTER III

FROM the thirteenth to the sixteenth centuries of the Christian era, as has been already noticed, Japan was occupied with the religious and political strife which preceded the unification of the Empire under the Tokugawa Shogunate (military rule). About 1600 A.D. Iyeyasu became the recognized Shogun (military ruler) of Japan, and from that time we enter upon an era of peace and culture. Iyeyasu saw that, in order to make peace permanent, the ideals of the people must be elevated, so he encouraged learning and education. His intention was to abandon the cruel ideals of the past, root out insincerity, and thus, by raising the public ideal, strengthen the hands of the government. During the reign of about half of the fifteen shoguns this ideal flourished and ethical teaching prevailed. The government patronized the teaching of Choo-he,[2] a Chinese scholar of the twelfth century, because of the great emphasis he laid upon obe-

[1] See also "Development of Japanese Religions," by Dr. G. W. Knox.

[2] Known in Japan as Shushi (1130–1200 A.D.).

dience. Such teaching suited the purpose of the government, and, as a result, the learning of the time was almost entirely Chinese, of one school or another. Things Chinese were very much prized.

The Choo-he learning had first been introduced by certain priests of Buddhism, who had gone to China to study. In the sixteenth century, when it became the orthodox learning of Japan, it was quite independent of Buddhism. Confucianism saw its best days in Japan after this revival of learning.

Choo-he scholars taught that "The Limitless" was without form or location, but was self-moving. In "The Great Limitless" they placed "The Great Limit," which was the original source from which all things sprang. "The Great Limit" is coequal with "The Great Limitless," which is not thought of as being prior to it in time. There was no real creation. "The Great Limit" began to move, and the great active or male principle was formed. Then when it ceased to move, the great passive or female principle was formed. The energy from these two forces is ever present in nature. By these forces were formed heaven and earth and all things which are regarded as modes of "The Great Limit." Of these modes man is the highest. These active and passive principles are principles of

"The Sensible World" ("Ki"), which corresponds
to all that can be perceived by the senses and is
divided into five elements — wood, fire, earth, metal,
and water. Immanent in all nature and binding
it together is the great source of all law and order
("Ri"),[1] "Reason." In thought this "Reason"
precedes nature and is found in its purest form
in man and "The Great Limitless." By obedience
to this law, we obtain human virtue. Man and
"The Great Limitless" are in nature essentially
the same. By birth man's nature is a perfect
mirror of "The Limitless," and when it is not cor-
rupted by "The Sensible World," but continues to
remain polished and bright, man is a sage.[2] In
addition to this real nature, man has a natural
disposition that is essentially made by "The
Sensible World." This "Law" or "Reason" is
that which gives whatever permanence and necessity there is in "The Sensible World." For example,
dogs, birds, barking and flying are all sensible, but
that dogs bark and birds fly is due to the great law,
Reason. The great question of dispute among
Japanese scholars of the Tokugawa age was the
relation of reason to the sensible world. The
Choo-he school held that both were found in

[1] Like the Greek "Logos" in that it may mean reason, truth,
law, or principle.
[2] This original nature is "Sei" in Japanese. A sage is Seijin,
Jin meaning man, *i.e.* a man in his real nature.

"The Great Limitless," and so it ends in a dualism.[1]

At first glance this teaching seems altogether foreign to our way of thinking, but in reality those men were seriously attempting to solve problems that are not unlike those which have perplexed scholars of all ages. If we leave out of account for the time being the ethical bearing of these teachings, the thought contained in "The Great Limitless" reminds us of interstellar ether, "The Great Limit" corresponds to nature, and "Ri" is the all-pervading law of the universe. But when we take into account the ethical application of their teaching, these problems become religious. For example, when we hear a Confucian scholar speak of "Heaven's Will" and say that "The essential quality of Heaven is Benevolence"; "Heaven is merciful to all men, so should we be"; "There is no falsehood in Heaven";[2] "Heaven is just three feet above a man's head," — we are led to conclude that they are dealing with the same problem that is contained in the "Ego" of Brahminism, the Absolute of Hegel, the Buddha of Ashvagosha, the Nameless One of Laou-tsze, and the God of the Christian.

[1] It resembles the familiar dualism, "God *vs*. the Universe."

[2] Cf. Transactions of the Asiatic Society of Japan, Vol. XXIV, Part IV. An article by Professor A. Lloyd, Professor of the Imperial University.

These Japanese scholars never questioned Confucius or Mencius, and their philosophy was received from Chinese scholars of the twelfth century. They were, even as Confucius himself, merely transmitters and interpreters without doing any very independent thinking. In spite of their limitations in thought, their mental training was exceedingly valuable, especially as they usually prided themselves in writing their ideas in classical Chinese too difficult for the people to grasp easily. Ninomiya did not like this class of scholars, particularly because he thought they were mere pedants, who were of no practical value to the state. In some respects this intellectual system, in its intolerance of the new and its loyalty to the old, resembled the contemporary learning of Europe. In fact it may be called the scholasticism of Japan.

In spite of the danger of being branded as heretics, and of being put under close guard, there were many great men in Japan who dared to differ from the orthodox school. Some of these formed "The Intuitional School," of Wang-Yang-Ming (1472–1528 A.D.), a Chinese scholar who was represented first in Japan by the great saint and scholar Nakae Toju, familiarly known as "The Sage of Omi," one of the most pious and thoughtful men of his age. This school laid great stress on morality — the practical life; and not on learning —

the speculative life. Practical morality was the only true learning. Reason and " The Sensible World " were but different aspects of one original substance. In this they were opposed to the dualism of Choo-he, and may be said to resemble modern Monists. This school, unlike the Choo-he school, made soul (literally, " heart ") and reason or truth one, and laid great stress on the purification of the soul as the most effectual means of attaining truth. Hence for them moral conduct was knowledge. In this they seemed to have taught the opposite to Socrates and Plato, who made knowledge virtue, meaning by knowledge speculative knowledge or philosophy. The Choo-he school laid more stress on speculative knowledge.

There was still another school of Confucianism in Japan, whose aim was to go back to the sages. The exponents of this school were great men, but their doctrines were not characterized by the uniformity and unity of the others. The founder of the school was Yamaga Soko [1] (born circa 1611 A.D.), one of the most famous teachers of Chinese learning and military tactics in Japanese history. He claimed that the other schools were not truly Confucian, and that he went directly to the sages

---

[1] This man taught the retainers of the lord Asano Takumi, famous for having the 47 retainers who avenged the death of their lord and then died by cutting out their own stomachs.

for his views. He thought that a man who really assimilated the learning of the sages would become benevolent, courageous, and, finally losing all ambition for success and fame, his one desire would be to follow truth. For him there was no beginning or end of the universe. Men and things were united with "heaven." He resembles Parmenides in that going and coming, development and decay, in one word, change was merely on the surface, but in essence there was no such thing. He laid great emphasis on learning being for true men to follow. It was practical and had to do with the trifling matters of every day. Our daily conduct is essential in learning. In other words, for him wisdom must be virtue.

After him came Ito Jinsai[1] (born circa 1628 A.D.), one of the most important representatives of the classical school. His idea of the kosmos was monistic and very much opposed to the dualism of the Choo-he scholars. He held that "Reason" ("Ri") came from "The Sensible World" ("Ki"). All things including heaven and earth have come from a non-spiritual "Ki," i.e. from "The Sensible World." This "Sensible World" is active, and in its movement it continually alternates between the

---

[1] I am indebted to my teacher, Mr. Komae, a graduate of The Imperial University, Tokyo, for his expositions of this school, and for the original quotations from the teachings of these men.

great male and female principles. Various existences spring from this movement of "The Sensible
World." He assumed that naturally there arose
an element of permanence in the midst of change,
which is natural to "Ki." In other words, "The
Sensible World" in its constant flux develops law,
which becomes the way of humanity. His theory
of the universe may be classified as a theory of
"Metaphysical Sensationalism." Once he has obtained the law, his theory resembles that of
Heraclitus. A few quotations from Ito's teaching
may help make clear his views. The kosmos is
one great living being. It has one generative
principle, but is itself not created. It is eternal.
There is no absolute birth and death for either men
or things. From the standpoint of non-existence
we cannot explain anything. There is no such
thing as nothing. He says that the heretical
school of Choo-he bases the universe on "Reason,"
i.e. permanence, but he himself bases it on "The
Sensible World," *i.e.* changing or flux, so that his
universe is all movement and activity. The attitude of the universe is always positive, according to this man. Things always grow or are born,
while death is merely change. Benevolence and
righteousness in the human way resemble the active
and passive principles of nature, apart from which
there is no way. Benevolence is involved in

righteousness as the active principle is involved
in the passive.

Still another school of this same classical type
was that of Ogiu Sorai, a contemporary of Ito
Jinsai. After the death of Confucius there was a
dispute as to whether man's essential nature was
evil or not. Sorai claimed that it was, and that
by music and propriety it would be remedied.
The Human Way (*i.e.* Human Virtue) is a general name for administration (*i.e.* the source of
law), propriety, music, and correction which were
the qualities discovered by the ancient kings.
Apart from these, there is no way. This is explained as follows: when men are born, desires
spring up; when they cannot realize their desires,
which are unlimited, struggle arises, followed by
confusion; when confusion arises, it causes suffering.
The ancient kings (*i.e.* administration) disliked
confusion, and made laws which determined propriety and righteousness. Then music and correction come in, as a means of culture for the soul that
is regarded as being evil. Sorai differed from Ito, in
that the way for him is a "Made Way" as just
outlined, and not one that is contained in the nature
of things. The ancients were very wise; receiving
"The will of heaven," they governed, feeling it
to be their duty to bring peace to earth. For
Sorai, the origin of "the way" was "the will of

heaven." At heaven's command Emperors are crowned, and retainers, officials, and subjects are chosen. Even as in a home there are found the master and his wife and children; when all agree with the master, there is peace, so the retainer agreeing with his lord fulfils his heavenly mission. In another place he says: "The ancient kings established the way in benevolence, therefore administration, propriety, music, and correction are benevolence. Unless a man is benevolent, he cannot give the people peace."

This, in very brief, is an account of the three schools of Confucianism in Japan at this time. It has not been my purpose to make it exhaustive, but rather to show some of the thought which was influencing the age with which Ninomiya was so closely identified.

CHAPTER IV

"TAOISM IN OUTLINE"

TAOISM has not had as important a place in Japan as Buddhism or Confucianism, although it is supposed to have been known since the time Confucianism entered Japan. The first real evidence of it in Japan was when Shotoku Taishi (circa 600 A.D.) issued a commentary on one of the sacred books of Buddhism, and quoted from Laou-tsze. But the teaching was eclipsed by Buddhism, and was looked upon as tending to Nihilism. The great Buddhist priest Kukai (circa 797 A.D.) was attracted by Taoism, and expounded the best parts of it in his book written before his first visit to China. He says: "The states of various existences differ; some fly, some live in water. So by different ways sages instruct the people. For example, there are Buddha, Laou-tsze, and Confucius." From this it is evident that Taoism was in Japan before 797 A.D., or before Kukai went to China.[1]

Taoism is the religion of the "Tao" way or truth, which is the nameless one behind all material form; itself formless, yet manifested in the "nameless

[1] Cf. "Outline of Philosophy in Japan," by Mr. Arima.

26

way," nature and man.[1] "It is intangible yet omnipresent, formless yet the source of all form, containing everything yet contained in all." The Tao is only understood at all by one's higher intuition, hence meditation and retirement are essential to purification of the spiritual life. Then Laou-tsze advises men to "Close the doors[2] of the senses; blunt the sharp; unravel the confused; harmonize the dazzling and become one with the all." This is the mystery of "Unity" by which he seems to mean that the profoundest truths of spiritual life are those inwardly experienced. The lotus[3] plant is used to illustrate the difference between the wise man of Taoism and the ordinary man. The latter, attracted by the leaves and especially by the flowers, wades into the water to get them, but is soon wallowing in the mire. The sage remains quietly on the bank, admiring and enjoying the beauty, without desiring to possess, and yet more truly possessing them than the other man whom he is able to assist. "The holy man, because he has no interests, is able to secure his interests."

The greatest good resembles water, which is able to benefit all things without asserting itself.

[1] Cf. "The Tao Teh King," translated by C. Spurgeon Medhurst, to which I am greatly indebted for this brief outline.

[2] "The Tao Teh King," by C. S. Medhurst, Chapter XVI.

[3] *Ibid.*, Chapter VI, page 3.

The man who comes near to "Tao" is able to benefit others, reform the community in which he lives, strengthen moral quality, and increase sincerity. Human development is from the animal filled with lust to the purity of the sage, whose centre is in "The One"; from a self-centred, discontented child to a god abiding in the peace and joy of the eternal. Man is never without some relation to "The Tao," but the perfect man or sage abides in "The Tao" and so is above fear, favor, disgrace, calamity.[1] "The five colors[2] blind men. The five tones[3] deafen men's ears. The five flavors[4] blunt men's appetites. On this account the holy man regards the stomach and not the eye." It is not unlike our saying, "Your eye is greedier than your heart."[5] The constant presence of this perfect ideal in the soul keeps men from error in thought, word, or conduct. Unlike Confucius, who tried to purify the state by law, Laou-tsze would purify it by a purification of the inner life. Laou-tsze adopted the simple life in order to contemplate "The Tao" without interruption.

[1] "The Tao Teh King," by C. S. Medhurst, Chapter XII, page 21.   [2] Blue, yellow, black, white, red.

[3] C, D, E, G, A.

[4] Sour, salt, sweet, tart, bitter.

[5] Cf. Medhurst. According to Wang Pi, "The stomach serves; therefore the sage disregards the eye." Another scholar says, "The eye covets more than it retains; the stomach desires no more than it requires."

CHAPTER V

THE supremacy of Chinese learning led men into a blind admiration for China and things Chinese. Men like Ogiu Sorai, in teaching their disciples, belittled Japanese learning, and exalted Chinese. Japanese loyalty and filial piety were thought by some to be threatened with destruction. Before he died Keichiu[1] began to call men back to things Japanese. A Shinto priest, Kada Adzuma-maro, ventured publicly to oppose this pro-Chinese tendency. He was a clever and wise man, who, while acquainted with Chinese literature, studied the ancient language and customs of Japan and read all the ancient rituals and collections of poetry, history, and law. He became a favorite of the eighth shogun and purposed to build a school in Kyoto for the study of the ancient classics of Japan. He said to the people: "There is one thing to be deplored. Japanese teaching has been handed down from the gods, but year after year

[1] I am indebted to my teacher, Mr. Hayashi of Kanazawa, for his assistance in translating the ideas contained in this outline.

29

the people are becoming more and more ignorant of it. Japanese books, ancient laws and institutions, have almost fallen into disuse, and the art of composing Japanese is almost lost. In Shintoism, those who speak do not know what they are talking about. In Chinese literature, our scholars are imitating Chinese scholars, or else they are talking nonsense only. From early times, I felt it my duty to attack heretical opinions, and with this in view I became educated. I feel that I must not cease till I recover the ancient way." He died in the first year of Genbun, 1715 A.D.

The work he had left undone was taken up by Kamo Mabuchi, a very accurate and deeply critical scholar of ancient learning. In order to make clear the ancient way, he studied all the ancient literature, but died before he had made his views public. He left many disciples, but none so famous as Motoori Norinaga, who was to bring the ancient learning to its consummation and accomplish the end for which all his predecessors had worked; viz. "To establish, instead of 'The Way of the Sages' as taught by Chinese scholars, 'The Great Way' of the gods kept unchangeable until now."

Motoori Norinaga was born in Ise, May 7, 1730 A.D. He was a great worker and left many books. A few quotations will give his ideas.

"To become learned, and know the great Truth, one must first remove the Chinese idea. Truth does not depend on learning. The inborn true heart is the truth." As opposed to the true heart he thus describes the Chinese heart: "The Chinese heart means not only liking the customs of China and respecting that country, but it is natural for it to criticise and discuss everything in the world. This all comes from the influence of Chinese books." "'The Way' was first inspired by the eternal deity and originated by Izanagi and Izanami, from whom Amaterasu[1] received it and kept it. Therefore since this way is the way of the gods, we must not mix profane ideas with it."

He rejected the Confucian idea of "Heavenly Will" and the Buddhist fate, and ascribed happiness and calamity to the different gods. He held that that which was not described by the ancient literature was miraculous and not to be discussed by profane lips. In other words, he had the idea that the ancient literature of Japan was verbally inspired, and that it was sacrilegious to subject it to literary criticism. This same attitude to the legends and myths of Shintoism has existed down to recent times. But scholars like Dr. Kume have dared

[1] Amaterasu is the Sun Goddess from whom the Imperial House descended.

to subject these sacred writings to higher criticism with good results, although they suffered for their opinions.

"In China, human calamity and happiness, peace and confusion, and a thousand other things are the work of heaven. They talk of 'heaven's way,' 'heaven's will,' 'heaven's reason,' making them most awe-inspiring and fearful. That is because the Chinese do not know that all things are in the providence of God. Therefore they have artificially invented a human way. Heaven is only the name of the place or country of the gods. Heaven has no will; such an idea is impossible. Instead of adoring and fearing God, they adored the palace but not the Emperor." "In China, they are not absolutely without a knowledge of God. Since they worship God, they probably have some idea of His truth, but they do not know that there are such gods in the world as first created the heavens and made all things. When they treat of such great things, they say 'Heaven,' but for lesser things, they say 'God.' Even the great Amaterasu is slighted by them. They are quite indifferent to her. I regret that they do not know that they must adore this goddess." "Our Imperial country is the great centre of all countries, and is their parent. Our just and true way has been given to us." "The true way is free from any human art, since it is just as God originated it. When Laou-tsze and Soshi[1] explained 'The way,' they disliked anything artificial. In this respect their teaching resembled the true way, but their doctrine was the product of their own intellect and not because they lived in Japan and heard of the 'Japanese True Way.' Since it is not the result of learning of the Japanese gods, they do not understand the true meaning of the great way. Therefore it is quite different from it. Japanese-Chinese scholars do not know the difference, so, if there is even a slight resemblance, they say the ways are the same, even though they are essentially different. This is very ridiculous." "If you ask what kind of way this is, I will answer that it is not a way that naturally exists in the universe. Neither is it a made way. I hesitate even to mention this way, depending as it does on our ancestral gods. It is called 'The way of the Gods' because Amaterasu received it from Izanagi and Izanami, and transmitted it to her descendants."

"It is the duty of a scholar to investigate this way of the gods. It is the way of a pedant to deviate from this way and to indulge in empty speculation. Apart from this there is no particular 'Way of the Gods.' It is the way of the gods to investigate the doings of the gods. In the

---

[1] Soshi was a Taoist scholar in China.

history of the gods there are many incomprehensible things. Therefore it is impossible to understand providence. It is well for us to believe it. The pedant has the bad habit of trying to understand the way by force." "All things in the world are mysterious because they are the work of the mysterious and miraculous gods. If, ignorant of this, we try to explain them by our shallow minds,[1] we are foolish. It is the habit of the Chinese to try to explain the mysterious in this way. They can explain anything, even that black is white, by speculation. If they meet a difficulty they cannot explain, they call it heaven. That is because they do not know of the existence of the gods."

Expressed in a modern form, this movement sought to emphasize the authority and value of what one might call revelation as opposed to human science and philosophy. Motoori may well be called the father of modern patriotism in Japan. His most distinguished disciple was Hirata Atsutane, the latest and, in some ways, the most admirable exponent of national religion of his day. Hirata is admired very much by the Japanese because of his intense loyalty to Japan and the Emperor. He knew something about the Bible

[1] Motoori's attitude to the legends of Shinto resembles the attitude of some toward the Bible. This becomes more evident if we substitute God for gods throughout these quotations.

and was slightly acquainted with astronomy and physical geography. This knowledge he received from the Dutch. His religious views resemble those of his teacher, Motoori Norinaga.

The influence of Confucian "Heaven," the Taoist "Way," the Buddhist "Law," and the Christian "God" on the polytheism of Japan has tended toward unity, and a movement of thought has gone on in Japan not unlike that which went on in Judea when the national god became not merely a god among other gods, but "The God" of all the earth. In modern times a Shinto scholar in Japan, named Kume, says frankly that "Shintoism[1] is monotheistic." The *Japan Mail* reported a conversation between Dr. Kume and several Shinto priests somewhat as follows: —

DR. KUME. "Religion may be monotheistic or polytheistic, but the latter is the lower form. Shinto in my view is monotheistic. If this were generally known, foreigners would be willing to worship at Ise, the Imperial Shrine."

THE PRIESTS. "You quoted with approval that the gods existed only in imagination, and yet you admit that our Emperor and the Japanese

---

[1] In 1899 Shintoism was secularized and ceased to be recognized as a religion. It became "merely a mechanism for keeping one generation in touch with another." It is now the embodiment of the national spirit of Japan, and all Japanese Christians should be loyal Shintoists, in this sense.

people descended from Amaterasu. Now how can an imaginary being have descendants?"

DR. KUME. "I meant that no god can be seen with the bodily eye."

THE PRIESTS. "We do not know what you mean by stating that Ise is not for Amaterasu in reality, but for the worship of heaven."

DR. KUME. "In the 'Kojiki'[1] it says Amaterasu gave a mirror with these words: 'You shall reverence this mirror as a symbol of my spirit.' Now, she meant not the soul of a dead person, but the divine essence which manifested itself in human beings."

THE PRIESTS. "You say 'Divine Essence'; do you mean as a foreigner means that God manifests Himself in man?"

DR. KUME. "Yes."

Besides Dr. Kume there have been others who have felt that Shintoism should become more truly modern in its idea. A Mr. Sakamoto Seitaku, about thirteen years ago, held that "The One Supreme[2] God," by means of His spirit, created other two[3] deities forming a trinity in unity, and from them were developed other spirits, including man.

Another sect of Shintoism known as Jikkokyo

---

[1] A record of ancient things in Japan.
[2] Ame-No-Mi-Naka-Nushi-No Kama
[3] Takami-Musubi, Kammi-Musubi.

36

founded in the sixteenth century aims at preaching peace and good-will. Its founder, Hasegawa Kakugyo, at the age of eighteen, was so distressed over the evils resulting from the civil strife of his day that he retired to a cave on Mount Fuji and constantly prayed for peace. He lived to see his prayers answered.

The teachings I have been outlining were largely confined to the samurai and higher classes until about 1750 A.D. The majority of teachers spoke in a language unknown to the common people. In 1739 A.D. Ishida Baigan was born. He became a humble clerk in a store, but spent his spare time in earnest study. When he thought the time ripe, he began to teach the merchant classes a popularized form of these teachings. He and his disciples were famous preachers in Japan. They advertised their lectures open to all and invited the common people to come without an introduction. Their teachings emphasize especially the five relations and the five cardinal virtues of Confucius. In 1787 Ninomiya Sontoku, who accomplished a similar work for the farmers, was born. These teachings had a great influence on his life and thought. His view of the universe was Confucian, and so his conception of the ancestral god of Japan was very much higher than the popular idea.

CHAPTER VI

LAND TENURE [1]

In order to understand the conditions of Nino-miya's time, it is necessary to give some idea of the method of holding land in ancient Japan. The original landowners of Japan were called "Goshi." After much strife the strongest of them, and in time nearly all of them, became territorial lords. This was probably the origin of the feudal system in Japan. Afterwards some feudal lords who disliked constant warfare became Goshi, retaining their standing as samurai. It is said that an old man who saved the Shogun's life was offered as a reward for his loyalty the privilege of becoming a daimio, but because he disliked war he declined the offer. The Shogun then presented him with all the land included in a wave of his cane and the title of Goshi. He received this land under the red seal of the Shogun, thus escaping from taxation.

Land owned by the Shogun was rented out to the farmers in small holdings.

[1] Cf. also Transactions of the Asiatic Society of Japan, Vol. XX, Part I; Vol. XX, Part II.

Various communities held land which was used for burying dead animals, for cemeteries, and for temple grounds, etc. Land held in this way could not be sold except with the consent of the villagers. In some places village land was cultivated by a class who resembled serfs. They lived in a common enclosure and ate from a common kitchen. Their presence was encouraged as a safeguard against robbers. In Japan, up to 700 A.D., serfs were transferred with the land when it was sold. In 676 A.D. private slaves were declared the property of the state. It was not until the beginning of Meiji (1871) that Hi-nin (outcasts) were given the rights of citizenship and first recognized as human beings.

Another class of landowners was the farmer-samurai, who cultivated his land in addition to rendering military service to his lord. He enjoyed more freedom than an ordinary samurai, because he did not live at the feudal castle. His standing was very high, and his servants were allowed to carry swords.

Large landowners sometimes had many tenants under them. The average farm in Japan is comparatively small, being between two and three acres. The average yield per acre is between thirty and forty bushels of grain. Sometimes a man in one farming community obtained land in another by foreclosing a mortgage. But as a rule the community paid the mortgage rather than suffer any such disgrace.

Laborers who went from their own community to obtain work in another were called "Water-drinking Farmers." If they became attached to the new lord, they were allowed to build a small house on the uncultivated hillside and transfer their names to the district office where they had chosen to live. Their children were regarded as regular tenants.

Landlords and tax-gatherers were expected to treat those under them with all consideration. If crops were bad, they must accept a rebate. In case of fire the rent was remitted for one hundred days in order to give the unfortunate man a chance to rebuild. Sometimes the landlord, when pressed by poverty, was not satisfied with the legitimate rent, but popular opinion was against methods of extortion. Landlords were expected to be generous, patient, and kind.

A district officer and several assistants had charge of all taxation. This officer was also expected to have the well-being of the people at heart, treating them with all justice and equity. He was to adjust boundaries, look after the water supply, repair dikes and embankments, investigate the cause of the failure of the crops, and advise as to the right seed to sow.

CHAPTER VII

MORAL AND ECONOMIC CONDITIONS OF NINOMIYA'S TIME [1]

THE Tokugawa government had ruled the Japanese Empire for nearly three centuries. The first part of this period was a time of prosperity, and the power of the Shogun was at its height. The government was very careful not to allow any teaching that might tend in any way to undermine its influence. Not only was Christianity forbidden, but men were prohibited to think or say anything that was opposed to the Choo-he school that had found favor in the eyes of the government. Those who were too big to keep their thoughts in air-tight compartments were punished with imprisonment or death, either as traitors or heretics. The latter part of the Tokugawa age was one of steady decline. To use a Japanese figure, the winds of decay were blowing over the feudal tree, and were shaking it to its very roots. The

[1] The material herein outlined is largely based on two Japanese books : —

(a) "Ninomiya Sontoku and his Influence," by Mr. Tomeoka.

(b) A Book given to our Orphanage by the Government in which was a History of Benevolent Work in Japan.

power of the Shogun[1] was lost and there was no hope of it ever being resuscitated.

This period of decline and social corruption, of change and decay, with all the struggle which it entailed, was the necessary condition of the achievements of the present age of progress in Japan. As we picture the social conditions of the age in which Ninomiya was born, we must not forget that underneath the apparent degeneration were the germs of the present age of progress, and that this progress has perhaps not had a parallel in any other nation in the same period of time. Such progress cannot be a mushroom growth; it has back of it a long history of preparation which has been an essential foundation of the modern. The last years of the Tokugawa period resembled those crises when prophets appear to call the people out of the ruts into which they had fallen. At such times evils, physical and social, have by no means an insignificant influence for good. In this sense the great famines of Tenmei Era (1781–1788 A.D.) and Tempo Era (1830–1844 A.D.) were not unmixed evils. They were like so much chastisement given by nature to enforce the lessons that the great teacher of the age, Ninomiya Sontoku, was trying to teach, when he emphasized the importance of morality, economy, and industry.

[1] Military ruler.

During the famine of Tenmei, it was customary for the poor to attack and destroy the houses of the rich. This was done in broad daylight, not so much for the purpose of thieving as to express the indignation of the people at the luxury and ease of the class by whom they were oppressed. Sadanobu Matsudaira put forth earnest efforts to rescue society from these conditions, and to some extent succeeded, for, during the reign of the eleventh shogun, Ienari, there was comparative peace, and the era was called the "Kansei No Kaikaku" — The Reformation of Kansei. It was also called the "Ogoshosama No Chisei" — the Reign of Ogoshosama. But this was not true peace, for the reformation of Matsudaira did not go deep enough. After his resignation, the people gradually relapsed into luxury and ease, and the government finances fell into a state of confusion. Mr. Hildreth speaks of the luxury of the merchant class of this time, and of their buying position with gold. A Japanese writer in this age says that even farmers and merchants were able to purchase the rank of samurai. The famines of the fourth and seventh year of Tempo Era (1833 and 1836) left the people in a wretched condition. It is said that many of them actually starved to death by the roadside, in spite of the efforts of the benevolent to save them. Rice was exceedingly dear;

the government frequently distributed it to the poor, and built homes for the homeless. At this time the former habit of housebreaking was not indulged in. The writer says that on the last night of the seventh year of Tempo Era (1836) he counted, from Yanagiwara Street to Asakusa, Mitsuke, over thirty persons who had starved to death on the street.

In the eighth year of the Tempo Era (1837) on the 19th of February, occurred what may be called the Heihachiro Riot. The mayor of Osaka was very tyrannical and did not attempt to help in reforming society, although it was brought to his attention that the rich were living in luxury and the poor were terribly oppressed. Oshiwo Heihachiro, who was so aroused at this time that he sold several hundred books, in order to raise funds to help the people, approached the mayor with a plan for relieving them, but received no sympathy. Oshiwo was so annoyed that he gathered a company, and, attacking the mayor's house, burnt it to the ground. Afterwards being overcome by government officials, he committed suicide.

In the eighth year of Tempo Era (1837) the Shogun, Ienari, resigned, and Ieyoshi succeeded him as the twelfth Shogun (a military ruler) and Mizu-no-Echizen-no-Kami Tadakuni became prime minister. The latter was a great man. He introduced many good reforms, to which are given the names, "Tempo No Shinsei," and "Mizu-Echi-No Kaikaku"—"The New Policy of Tempo," and "The Reformation of Mizu-no-Echizen." Though well meaning, he at length went to such extremes that he counteracted the good he might otherwise have accomplished. He insisted on such extreme economy, and enforced his commandments with such severity, that a reaction set in against him, and he was dismissed from office by the Shogun, on the ground that he was not satisfactory for business. His successor was Abe Masahiro.

The social conditions of this time were such that they are not pleasant to describe; a popular song intimated that the men who were popular were profligate, winebibbers, lovers of women, lovers of luxury, speculators. They flattered others and demeaned themselves to win favor. They did not take life seriously. Officials, accomplished in military arts and learning, men who were faithful and honest, were often not admired in this age. Another song describes the age as follows: "In the world, it is true; it is reasonable. What is true? I don't know exactly." The force of which polite expressions is, that men were afraid of being punished for independence of thought; they were exceedingly patronizing.

In ancient times when merchants and farmers

went to the houses of ill fame, they were accustomed to go to an inn, and, when they were the worse of liquor, they would cover their heads with a deep umbrella, and go in disguise. But at this time even the samurai were so degenerated that they did not hesitate to go even in broad daylight. They dressed in gay attire and went without any attempt at concealment. In "The History of the Fifteen Shoguns" the state of society is described. The temples and shrines were usually placed in unfenced wastes, in order to avoid taxation. In these waste places unlicensed prostitute houses were even more prosperous than the licensed quarters. The government finally abolished them and ordered that their inmates should remove to the licensed places or disband. In addition to the "yoshiwara" (licensed quarters) there were twenty-three places of this kind. The houses numbered 574, and the inmates who were not licensed, 4181. These were abolished by the efforts of Mizu-no-Echizen.

As might be expected from the prevalence of prostitution, there were many idlers in Japan at this time. The great famines referred to produced many starving people, and from the middle classes down there was much suffering. Rice became very dear, and other food was proportionately expensive. From the time of Tanuma the people had given themselves over to luxury. As a consequence the fields and mountains were deserted, and the people, even the farmers, were all flocking to the cities and towns. The villages were unoccupied, and the cities were crowded with idlers and criminals, so that even life was not safe.

A quotation from "To Sempu Ron," by Mr. Hoashi, describes the state of the people in the time of the twelfth Shogun : "Upland farms were difficult to cultivate; they required about three times as much labor in cultivation as the low-water fields, and yet they only produced about half as much grain. As a result, the upland farm villages were in very hard circumstances." Mr. Hoashi recommended that these fields should be irrigated as an important step toward governing the people.

He says, further, that during the three hundred years of peace the people had become pleasure-loving and neglectful, the mountain villages had become depopulated, and the great cities and feudal towns crowded. He says that this was not good, that it would have been better to have limited the number entering the cities, and that were this not done, cities and towns alone would grow and villages become deserted. When farmers rush to the cities, there is danger. Mr. Tomeoka says that when the country population rushes to the city, we have the first evidence of luxury. Luxury finally destroys the body of the people. The whole country becomes affected.

Mr. Hoashi thus described the neglect of religion at this time: "There were over 100,000 Buddhist temples in Japan, and many hundred thousand priests, of whom only a very few were educated. Little or no qualification was required to fill the office of head priest in a temple. Every temple had sufficient property to make ample provision for its priests. All the people had to be registered in a Buddhist temple, so that the membership neither increased nor decreased. Consequently the priests became careless in the performance of their duties and neglected study. The sons of the rich rarely became priests, and the ranks became filled with poor people who sought to escape the press of poverty. The character of the priests was naturally not good, and in this way Buddhism was rather a hindrance than a help to Japan. The conduct of the priests was so bad that in the eleventh year of Tempo Era (1840), in February, an edict was issued to correct the conduct of Buddhist priests. They were accustomed to ask for presents and money from the people, to live in extreme luxury, employ many servants, and use fine furniture." When a priest resigned in favor of his son, a great feast was made, and skilled artists were employed to draw pictures. Besides, the priests

48

were very impolite to the poor. Such luxury and conduct did not become Buddhists, so they were commanded to mend their ways.

The priests of Buddha's time wore clothes made from rags which had been discarded by sick people. They had no dwelling, but weathered the rain and wind, sometimes living under bridges and eating what the people placed in their bowls. In the age we are describing they were arrogant, luxury-loving and selfish, possessing land and living in state like noblemen.

When Matsudaira and Mizu-no-Echizen-no Kami attempted to reform these conditions, a series of edicts was issued. In the fourth year of Bunsei (1821) in November, an edict was issued condemning the customary magnificent and luxurious funerals. Two years later in September another was issued to the officials of the Tokugawa estate. It stated that the expense of the Tokugawa government was very great, notwithstanding the fact that the Tokugawa family were economical. The relatives of the family wished to repair their estates, but were embarrassed by lack of funds. It was therefore requested that the various offices should be more economical. During the ninth year of Tempo Era (1838) five edicts were issued in less than two months. One on April the 6th drew attention to the fact that the economical improvement in the people was only on the surface; that the people were not in good circumstances, and that they were neglectful of their duty. It placed the blame on the officials, and called on them to economize in clothes, wedding ceremonies, and other feasts, in building and furnishing their houses, and in servants, and it closed with an appeal to them to set an example to the lower classes. Another on April the 10th drew attention to former edicts against luxury; these had failed to improve the condition of the people, who were really living in poverty. It appealed to them to economize, as the western part of the castle had been burned and the Tokugawa family, in spite of their economical method of living, were in need of money; it granted permission to the people and their servants to wear inferior clothes for a period of three years in order to avoid useless expense. On April the 23d the use of gold and silver in combs, hairpins, tobacco pouches, pipes, purses, and toys was forbidden. Merchants and farmers were even forbidden to use those which had been handed down in their families for generations, except when they used them in the employ of the samurai. Merchants were given one year to dispose of such goods as they had on hand. On the 22d of May another edict called attention to certain extravagance in clothing and hair dress by the merchants, and ordered them to adopt the economical methods of the Tokugawa family, or be punished. These edicts made a great impression on the people, for in the thirteenth year of Tempo Era (1842) an edict was issued which indicates that the people hesitated to build new houses or repair old ones. It encouraged them to do works of necessity. Later on in the same year another edict drew attention to the fact that farmers had been using oil on their hair, and tying their cues with cord instead of straw. Instead of using their straw raincoats, they had adopted more expensive ones. Because of these bad customs they were unable to support their ancestral estates, and had in many cases become wine merchants. Therefore young men were tempted to drink. Old customs were being lost, and farming was neglected. Farmers were forbidden to become merchants.

The Japanese at this time were letting the Hollanders and other foreigners carry off their gold and copper, and were satisfied to receive in exchange nothing of any real value. Mr. Murdock[1] quotes Arai Hakuseki as saying even as early as 1708: "I compute the annual exportation of gold at about 15,000 kobans (30s.) so that in ten years this country is drained of 1,500,000 kobans, or £2,250,-000. With the exception of medicines we can dis-

[1] Cf. "A History of Japan," by Mr. Murdock, Vol. I, page 18.

pense with everything that is brought to us from abroad. The stuffs and other foreign commodities are of no real benefit to us. All the gold, silver, and copper extracted from the mines during the sway of Iyeyasu and since his time are gone, and, what is still more to be regretted, for things we could very well do without." Mr. Murdock says that the calculation is wild, but the argument sound. We may sometimes have reason to complain about the veracity of the Japanese merchant to-day, but where is there less conscience than in the treatment of men like the Japanese of this era or the North American Indians of the last century by Western seekers after gold?

Another indication of the poverty of the age in which Ninomiya was born was the fact that their coinage was debased. When the Dutch began to trade with Japan at the beginning of the seventeenth century, the gold koban was bought for six taels. At the end of the century the amount of gold in the coin was reduced to two-thirds of its original quantity.

During the centuries of isolation, it was necessary to emphasize the importance of agriculture. Because of the large population and the comparatively small area of arable land, it was very important that every foot of soil should be made to produce as much as possible. Consequently, a very unique system of irrigating and fertilizing was adopted from ancient times. Japanese farms are like so many gardens, in which not only vegetables, but grains of all kinds, are cared for, as our gardeners care for flowers. Consequently, the soil must be maintained by artificial means. But during the age we have been describing the government had lost its power, and the people had become indolent and luxury-loving. Their former careful methods of farming were neglected, and large tracts of land became deserted. The immorality and indolence of the people were written on the soil, and the result was famine after famine.

Mr. Murdock [1] in his new history points out that about 14,000 or 15,000 square miles of arable land had to support a population of 30,000,000, or nearly 2000 to the square mile. The Japanese not being meat eaters or milk-drinkers, the people, with the exception of the fishermen, had to depend on the crops; these sometimes failed and, as a result, the population of Japan was very often in sore distress. Instead of increasing at the rate of one and one-third per cent per annum as at present, it only increased at the rate of two and one-half per cent per century at this time (*i.e.* between 1721 and 1846 A.D.).

[1] Cf. Introduction, "A History of Japan," James Murdock.

CHAPTER VIII

ATTEMPTS TO IMPROVE THE CONDITION OF THE PEOPLE

THE history of these times would not be complete without some reference to the earnest attempts that were made to rescue the poor and relieve the distressed. Even as early as the seventh year of Kyoho Era (1722) the eighth Shogun, acting on the advice of the city doctor, Shozen, built a hospital for the poor in Koishikawa, near the site of the botanical gardens. Here roots were grown for medicine; food, clothing, bedding, and other necessaries were provided for the poor, who were allowed to remain in the institution eight months if their physical condition required it.

Miura Baien, a scholar of Tominaga, Bungo province, Kiushiu, in addition to assisting poor students with money and food, united, in the sixth year of Horeki (1756), with his fellow-villagers in what he called a "Jihi Mujin," a kind of benevolent association. The nature of this society may be judged from the following quotations: "If there is good fortune in a village, the villagers all rejoice together; if disaster, they all lament together. They are like brothers dwelling together. They unite to help the sick and the poor and, in case of quarrel, to make peace; when any one is guilty of bad conduct, they all advise together. In such a village peace will naturally prevail."

"The man born in poverty, in the morning starving, and in the evening freezing, naturally turns to evil. There is a saying, 'Poverty makes thieves.' But if men are diligent in their business, this evil spirit will die out, and the spirit of mercy will thrive." "The man who is diligent in business, and economical, and yet suffers want on account of sickness, or large family connection, or loss by theft, fire, or flood, is an honest, poor man and is deserving of our sympathy and help. Moreover, if we put ourselves in the place of the childless, the aged, the orphan, the dependent, the sickly, who are without food and shelter, we will have great sympathy for them, for we will then feel how sad is their condition. We will divide our food with them for at least half a day, and we will divide our hot water and warm their stomachs for at least one morning (*i.e.* we will share equally with them). We will do our utmost for them." "Many hands working together will soon accumulate a hill of dirt. So if we unite the people of a village, and gather what they may have to spare from their living, even if we relieve but a little distress, it is a great mercy to the poor, and very little sacrifice on our part."

This great man gave the villagers the following rules: "The head of each house shall urge upon his family the principles illustrated in the foregoing quotations. Old and young men and women shall bring to the club according to their means barley in summer, rice in autumn, and money in winter. The stewards of the club shall meet without fail every year, count the money, and examine the books. The money may then be loaned through the village authorities. The interest and principal shall be allowed to accumulate. Money shall not be loaned without good security. The funds shall be allowed to accumulate before any loans are made. Subscriptions shall not be forced. The money shall be called 'Shujin-no-nai-Kane' (No-Master-Money), and shall be distributed by the stewards in consultation with the village officials, to the most needy first, and afterwards to others in proportion to their need. No one person shall be allowed to use the money freely. Applicants whose characters display filial love, chastity, and loyalty may receive help. Partiality shall be avoided. Subscriptions above ten momme (about one and a quarter ounces) of silver and one 'to' (about four gallons) of rice shall entitle the donors to enrolment." This system continued to exist until the first year of Meiji (1868 A.D.).

Sato Issai (1772–1859) had an elaborate scheme extending over twenty years, for providing stores of rice against famine.

Many of the great scholars and some of the feudal lords were very earnest in their efforts for the people. Matsudaira Sadanobu (1758–1829), lord of Shirakawa, was such a wise administrator that during the Tenmei famine his province was comparatively free from distress. Afterwards he was made minister of the Tokugawa government and became a great benefactor in the city of Yedo, which had suffered much during the famine. In the fourth year of Kansei (1792) when he established the "Machi-kwaisho," he saved from the city expense about 37,000 ryo,[1] of which 25,900 ryo was donated to the relief fund of the city. In the seventh year of Meiji (1847 A.D.) about 1,700,-000 ryo was delivered to the city of Tokyo, and was used in the construction of public works, while the Tokyo Fu building, The Higher Commercial School, and the "Yoikuiin," an institution for caring for helpless old people and children, were first established from this fund. Matsudaira also established a great reformatory known as "Ninsoku-

[1] The value of ancient money is very difficult to obtain, because it is relative. One ryo is now worth about five dollars.

Yoseba." This institution was intended to help ex-prisoners, who on their release from jail were homeless and without means of support. Here, carpenters, joiners, lacquerers, rice-cleaners, farmers, and others worked usually from eight A.M. until four P.M. receiving their respective wages, part of which was reserved as a surplus fund for future use. At first the average attendance in the institution was 135, but in the second year of Kokka (1845) it rose as high as 600.

Uesugi Yozan (1750–1822) was another admirable man. He was an adopted son of the Uesugi family. After his adoption his first act was to go to a shrine, and proclaim himself in favor of the simple life. He issued an edict prohibiting gambling; he encouraged the people to be industrious, and to cultivate the deserted places. In this way he was successful in restoring the fallen fortunes of the estate, paying off all the debts, and providing against famine. When the neighboring provinces were reduced to such straits that some of them even resorted to eating the flesh of their dead companions, Yozan's province had enough and to spare.

Hosokawa Shigekata (1718–1755), lord of Higo in Kiushiu, and Tokugawa Harusada, of Kii province, were so benevolent that the people said, "In Kiushiu there is a 'Kirin' and in Higo there is a 'Hoo.'" Both of these are fabulous creations that would not hurt a living thing, not even a plant. The former lord is said to have sacrificed personal comforts in order to be able to save his people. He had ninety-seven centres for storing and distributing rice.

Tsugaru Nobuaki of Oshiu not only opened up storehouses, but gave his private funds to help the poor. He was accustomed to reward farmers who were specially industrious in breaking up barren wastes. He required every village chief to build a storehouse for rice. He ordered his soldiers, in their leisure, to cultivate the land.

We might mention the artist priest, Gessen, of the Jodo sect, in Ise, who, when dying, sent his accumulated wealth to the government to feed the poor; also the merchant Kumagai Naoyasu of Kyoto, who, during one of the famines, spent all his fortune, and even sold his land that he might help the poor. Many others from all parts of Japan lived, labored, and sacrificed for their fellowmen, and it is not unnatural to suppose that their lives and deeds were an inspiration to Ninomiya in his great life work of service. Ninomiya, like the men we have mentioned, was exceedingly practical. Mr. Tomeoka says that he was the ideal of the practical. His perspiration was to him the water of baptism, and his sacred teachings were hidden in practical work. His genius was certainly called forth by the needs of his day.

CHAPTER IX

DURING the lifetime of Ninomiya, Japanese statesmen were perplexed to know what to do in regard to foreign intercourse. Western ships were constantly passing. When Ninomiya was six years old (1792), Russian ironclads came to the Hokkaido, and in the first year of Bunka (1804) a Russian ambassador arrived at Nagasaki, with an official message from the Czar. Two years later, two Russian ships called at Kabafuto, burned the homes of the people, captured four Japanese, and carried off much rice, salt, and wine. In August, 1808, an English ship came thirty ri (about seventy-three miles) from Nagasaki. In 1853 Commodore Perry came with four war vessels and five hundred blue-jackets to Uraga, near Yokosuka, and in the same year four Russian ironclads came to Nagasaki. In August of that year the Tokugawa government ordered eleven forts built in Shinagawa Bay, near Tokyo, and Egawa Torozaemon was intrusted with this work. The following year Commodore Perry again called, and demanded that Japan should fulfil her promise to trade with the West. In the third year of Ansei (1856) Townsend Harris came to Shimada in the interest of the United States of America. He was invited to Yedo, for consultation in regard to the treaties. In the fifth year of Ansei (1858), Ii Naosuke was prime minister. He opened up five ports to foreign trade, and established treaties with the United States of America, Russia, England, Holland, Portugal, and Germany. This cost him his life, for he was killed by the Ronins of Mito at the gate of Sakurada. Ii Naosuke was a great patriot, who, though intensely anxious for his country and her glory, saw that true patriotism is to be realized in the cosmopolitan spirit that some of the Mito class of patriots are even yet so afraid of advocating. Ii Naosuke's little poem, translated by Sir Ernest Satow, shows the intense patriotism of this great statesman: —

> "As beats the ceaseless wave on Omi's strand,
>   So breaks my heart for our beloved land."

This great question of opening up the country was constantly in the minds of the people of Ninomiya's time. Some favored the proposition and were punished by the Tokugawa government for their liberal views. In the eighth year of Bunsei (1825) it was even decided to fire, without hesitation, on all foreign ships. This spirit of opposition continued to exist up to the time of the treaties. The great Matsudaira of whom we have already spoken expressed himself [1] on the coming of the foreign ship. He drew a black ship and wrote above it, "Remembering, even while we sleep, that such ships will come is a treasure to Japan." He thought that the coming of these ships was a warning to Japan to prepare to defend her coasts.

This, in brief, was the condition of Japan when Ninomiya began his great work. The feudal system was much the same as the feudal system in any other country. Raisanyo, a contemporary of Matsudaira Sadanobu, said: "As the feudal system becomes stronger, caste becomes more and more firmly fixed; even excellent men cannot stretch out their feet. There is no freedom, no people's rights, the cloud of oppression prevails." And yet, Ninomiya, a poor farmer, who made the best of his opportunities, was able, in spite of these conditions, to rise, until to-day he is not only

[1] Literally, a poem. Japanese poetry is constructed according to certain fixed forms known by most Japanese students. The practice of making poems is very common. In some schools they meet in poetical societies for this purpose. Every New Year the Emperor announces a subject for a poem competition. As the best ten of these poems are read by H. I. Majesty, there are many competitors. While there are some long poems, the usual length is thirty-one syllables. Sometimes only seventeen syllables are used. When translated into English, I have called them sayings rather than poems.

studied and respected, but the students of his nation worship at his shrine. He came when things seemed to have reached a climax, and by his economic and ethical principles began a work that is still going on. He saw to some extent the importance of the moral, and sought to impress on the people at least part of the truth that Christ made uppermost when He said, "Seek ye first the Kingdom of God and His righteousness; and all these things shall be added unto you."

CHAPTER X

JAPANESE scholars have discussed the life and teaching of Ninomiya from various standpoints. Dr. Nakajima says that his teaching may be called "Ethical-Economy or Economic-Ethics." He draws attention to the fact that Ninomiya exalted industry and economy in an age when it was beneath the dignity of a gentleman to work. He thinks that his ethics resemble the thought of T. H. Green; and that his emphasis on sincerity is not altogether unlike Green's self-realization. He thinks that the influence of the teaching of this sage will be against the gambling of the present age, and also against the tendency to teach boys to be heroes, with the result that if they fail they become sullen, discontented, and pessimistic. Better teach them the necessity of being industrious and useful citizens.

Dr. Inoue Tetsujiro points out that Ninomiya, unlike scholars of rank and position, was a farmer from a humble home, who studied without a

64

teacher, and yet became a great leader. He suggests that there has not been any such man in Japan, and that Ninomiya might well be held up by the Educational Society of Japan as an example for Japanese boys. He compares him with Confucius, who, though a great teacher of morals, held views on economy. Ninomiya resembled Confucius in being born poor, and in being self-educated. He likens the "Evening Addresses" of Ninomiya to the "Analects of Confucius," both being a compilation of addresses without classification or system. He says that practically Ninomiya is a utilitarian, although his chief motive was not happiness, but sincerity. In his attitude to Buddhism, Confucianism, and Shintoism, he is an eclectic; he accepts anything good from any source, laying most stress on Confucianism, but in exceptional cases appealing to Buddhism. Although he did not like secular Shintoism, he emphasized the spirit of reverence for the ancient myths and ancestral worship.

Dr. Inoue thinks that Ninomiya resembles Christ, in that he sacrificed his life for the salvation of the people, and that after his death a society was formed. They were not alike, he thinks, in that, while Christ sacrificed His life for humanity, He denied the right to accumulate property. On the other hand, economy was the great object of Nino-

miya.   He says also that the "Life of Ninomiya"
and his "Evening Addresses" resemble the Gos-
pels and are as suitable for farmers as the Bible is
for Christians.   But he goes on to point out that
the teaching of Ninomiya must be changed to fit
the conditions of the present age, as they are not
suited to merchants.   Since Ninomiya's time commerce has developed; great trusts have been organized, debts accumulated, and money has been
borrowed from foreign countries, so that Ninomiya's opinions must be enlarged.

Dr. Kato,[1] ex-president of the Imperial University, says that Ninomiya's ideas of good and
evil resemble those of Thomas Hobbes.   Good
and evil are not the product of heaven, but of
human effort.   He says there have been many
great men in Japan who emphasized economy, but
neglected ethics.   Ninomiya differs from the others
in basing economy on morality.   If people had
understood Ninomiya, his success would have been
greater.

[1] Dr. Kato has been described to me as the "Japanese Haeckel."

CHAPTER XI

DR. INOUE also points out that personality has not been developed in the Orient even in Buddhism, Confucianism, or Bushido. The idea of individuality came from the West. While it is found to some extent in Confucianism, it is not clear-cut. It was not until recent times that Mr. Fukuzawa emphasized "independent self-respect." Ninomiya, however, in his appreciation of the value of the individual, resembles Western thought. Dr. Inoue thinks it a very remarkable thing that he should emphasize this idea, even in his time; to a foreigner looking at the life of Ninomiya there is nothing remarkable in the emphasis he lays on the importance of the individual. The events that went to make him great naturally developed his idea of individuality, even though he had not read of the teaching in Western books. But it was not impossible for some ideas of the West to have crept in through books that were being translated from the Dutch. Even as early as the Era of Kai (1624–1643 A.D.) Nonaka Kenzan sent messengers

67

yearly to Nagasaki and bought foreign books; these he translated and gave to his disciples, who applied the teaching in a very practical way; cultivating the mountains and fields, organizing the farmers into soldiers, and exhorting them to be industrious.

Mr. Murdock points out that in the reign of the eighth Shogun (1717–1745), who was so wise and gathered so many wise retainers that he is called "The Excellent Lord of the Middle Shogunate," a very active interest in Dutch literature was encouraged. Up to this time a very strict censorship had been kept on Dutch learning. The interpreters of Nagasaki now presented a petition to the Shogun for the privilege of studying the written language. Their request was granted. When the Shogun heard of their success, he desired to see a Dutch book. He was so pleased with the illustrations that he appointed two men to read the book.

About this time a Japanese [1] physician, Mayeda Riotaku, and two companions obtained Dutch books on anatomy. They went to the execution grounds to have the executioner dissect the body of a criminal in order that they might learn whether the Dutch medical science or their own was correct. This was the beginning of many such lessons.

[1] Cf. Transactions of the Asiatic Society of Japan, Vol. V, Part I.

Finally one of them decided to risk his life for the sake of science by publishing what they had thus discovered. Contrary to all expectation, the book was received even by the Shogun.

From this time the study of Dutch made great progress. The laws of nature, "History of Europe," and other books of that character prepared the people for the coming of Commodore Perry. By the beginning of the nineteenth century the government had official translators for Dutch books. In fact, several scholars were punished for translating and making public what the government thought unwise. Mr. Murdock says that the Dutch were kept in Deshima to play for Japan the part which Bacon's [1] "Merchants of Light" did for his utopian "New Atlantis," and that while the government wished for the light, they desired to control the meter, that there might be no risk of disastrous explosions.

In a speech at one of his garden parties, Count Okuma said, "Although I have no religion, I have notions in reference to a power that is above; these I received from the study of the Dutch books and physics." In view of these things it is not at all impossible that Ninomiya was influenced in his ideas of individuality by the West. But even if

[1] Cf. Bacon's "New Atlantis," page 136, in "Ideal Commonwealths," published in the World's Great Classic Series.

he were not so influenced, reflection on his own struggles and successes would give him a clear idea of the value of individuality, for he was "A golden son born from an iron father." But in any case, just as coal is the production from old trees, so the teachings of Ninomiya have largely come from older scholars and philanthropists.

PART I

THE LIFE OF NINOMIYA SONTOKU

CHAPTER I

THE EARLY YEARS OF NINOMIYA SONTOKU

NINOMIYA SONTOKU[1] is the most famous man
Japan has given to the industrial world. Every
Japanese schoolboy knows him by the name of
Kinjiro.[2]   He was born in 1787 in the village of
Kayama, near Mount Fuji, in the province of Sag-
ami.   He died in 1856, about a year after the sec-
ond visit of Commodore Perry to Japan.

His father was born of very well-to-do parents,
but, being a warm-hearted man, he spent almost all
his fortune on the poor.   When Kinjiro was born,
the family were really in hard straits.   To add
to their distress, when Kinjiro was five years old,
the Sa River overflowed its banks and washed
away his father's land, leaving them in abject
poverty.   When he was fourteen years old, his
father died.   His mother was forced to part with

---

[1] The materials for this life of Ninomiya are in effect translations from "Hotokuki," the authorized life of Ninomiya by his
greatest disciple, Mr. Takayoshi Tomida, and also free translations
from Mr. Tomeoka's "Anecdotes of Ninomiya."

[2] Kinjiro was his boyhood name.   It is not uncommon for Japanese to have several names.

her youngest child, but, after doing so, the poor woman was nearly heart-broken, and could not sleep. Kinjiro, seeing his mother's grief, offered to help her if she would take back the child. He said, "I will help you to bring him up, and I will work as hard as I can."

Even at the early age of twelve, when his father was too sick to work, Kinjiro took his father's place in rebuilding the river bank. When any of the men helped him in his task, in return he made straw sandals for them. When his father died, he became the main support of the family. He used to go to the hills to gather fagots, which he would sell, and with the proceeds buy the necessities of life. On these trips he was accustomed to carry the book which he was studying with him, so that, although a mere boy, he acquired a deep thirst for learning, and took every opportunity to study and to improve himself.

Many stories are told of those early years, the most interesting of which is his conversation with a Buddhist priest. When he was fourteen years of age, he went to a neighboring temple to pay his sick father's respects to the goddess Kwannon.[1]

[1] "The Goddess of Mercy, who is sometimes represented as having eleven faces and a thousand hands." These represent her bountiful spirit of mercy. In some old Japanese books every act of mercy is represented as the incarnation of this goddess, the Goddess of Mercy symbolized by the idol.

First Steps to Success — Hard Work and Study.

When there, he saw a priest reading one of the Buddhist sutras. Kinjiro overheard him, and to his surprise and delight was able to understand the meaning of it, so he drew near and asked the priest to read it over again, giving him two sen for his trouble. The priest looked surprised and amused, and gladly repeated it. Kinjiro was very much delighted, and returned to his home in high spirits. Shortly after this, he visited the old priest of his native village, and told him what he had heard. The old man was very much pleased, and said: "I am now over seventy years of age, and have never understood the meaning of those words at all, but you, a mere boy, can understand them. There is a brilliant future for you. Come, pray be my successor in this temple." Kinjiro replied that he was the eldest son in his own home, and that he must make the name of his father's house great and famous.

When Kinjiro was about twelve years of age, he went to work for a year with a farmer in the neighborhood. At the end of the year, before starting for home, he received, in addition to his board and lodging, a Japanese kimono and about two yen.[1] His mother expected him early and was waiting for him, but when at night he had not returned, she became quite anxious. Shortly after dark he

[1] One yen is about 50 cents.

came rushing in, all out of breath, and full of excitement. When his mother reproved him for being late, he told her that in the morning he had received from his master a kimono and two yen, and had immediately set out for home. On the way he had met a man with a lot of little pine trees [1] for sale. The poor man was very disheartened, because he had not succeeded in selling a single tree, and told Kinjiro that unless he could find a buyer he would be very much distressed. Kinjiro was sorry for the man, and an idea struck him whereby he could not only help the man, but could at the same time do the whole community a good service. As we already know, the Sa River sometimes overflowed its banks. Kinjiro thought if a couple of rows of pine trees were planted along the banks of the river, and once took root, it would remedy this difficulty. So he bought all the trees and spent the remainder of the day planting them. He felt sure his work would have its reward. To-day those trees are large, and not only support the river bank, but add much to the beauty of the scenery. They stand as a living monument of little Kinjiro's thoughtfulness.

When Kinjiro was working for the farmer, he was so poor that he could not buy paper, brush,

---

[1] The Japanese are conserving their forests. It is not unusual to see thousands of little trees being cultivated.

NINOMIYA MAKING STRAW SANDALS.

NINOMIYA WORKING ON THE RIVER BANK.

and ink to practise the Chinese characters, so he procured an old tray, filled it with very fine sand from the river-bed, and with a chopstick practised writing in the sand. As might be expected, he had no opportunity to go to school. The Buddhist priest of Zenrenji temple used to gather the poor boys and teach them reading and writing. Ninomiya was so busy that he could only attend on rainy days or rest days. At one of those gatherings, the boy sitting next him brought a sheet of blank paper. Kinjiro asked him if he would let him write a few Chinese characters on it. The boy gladly consented, and watched Kinjiro as he wrote, "Learn one character every day, and in one year you will know 365 characters, you young rascal." This has been called "The Three Hundred and Sixty-Five Day Maxim."

Kinjiro's constant anxiety lest the Sa River should again overflow was shared by all the people of the village. If they were not very careful every spring, the bank was in danger of breaking away. Kinjiro knew if a small opening were made, all would quickly give way, and so, in times of danger, he was constantly prowling around the dike repairing weak places, and removing anything that might make a hole in it. This became so noticeable that people were accustomed to say, "If you want to find Kinjiro, go to the dike." He was known by the villagers as "Dote Bozu" — dike priest.

As a boy he acquired two other nicknames. It is the custom of Japanese peasants to hull grain in a large wooden bowl, about two feet high. They walk round and round this bowl, pounding the grain with a heavy, long-handled mallet. When Kinjiro was employed in this way, he used to place a copy of one of his Confucian classics on a stand near the bowl. Every time as he went around the bowl, past the stand, he read a sentence. He would do this for hours at a time, day after day, if he happened to be doing that kind of work. In this way he got the nickname "Gururi Ippen," which means "once around."

He was also called "Crazy Kinjiro." Okabe Zenyemon, a wealthy man of the village, had in his employ a Confucian teacher, who occasionally gave public lectures on the sacred books. Kinjiro used to listen to him through the paper doors.[1] One day he surprised both the teacher and his audience, by crying out, "That is a mistake." The teacher was very angry, and opening the door

[1] A Japanese house has usually two sets of doors : the outer ones are wooden and are called rain doors ; the inner ones are light frames covered with translucent white paper. These sliding doors usually extend along the whole side of the house, running in grooves. The wooden doors are left open during the day and closed at night and during a storm.

to see who the intruder might be, discovered "Crazy Kinjiro." When he began to scold, the boy replied by very cleverly pointing out how he had been contradicting himself in his statements. The teacher was generous enough to admit the reasonableness of the boy's explanation, and was so impressed by his knowledge and understanding of Confucian teaching, that he afterwards frequently consulted Kinjiro as to the meaning and application of the same.

One time there was an historical story-teller in the village, reciting the story of Hideyoshi, an ancient warrior sometimes called the Napoleon of Japan. The audience was very much interested in the recital, when suddenly some one in the crowd applauded so boisterously that the singer became stage-struck, and could not proceed with the story. The people were very much annoyed, but on inquiring who the disturber was, found it was "Crazy Kinjiro." They said that it was useless to scold him, nevertheless the story-teller insisted upon meeting him the next day. Kinjiro's explanation was that it was far from his intention to disturb, but he thought the story lacked animation and expression, and that a little hearty applause might liven it up. It is said that the incident had a very beneficial effect upon the story-teller.

Another interesting story is told of these early

days at home. Kinjiro and his younger brother, Saburo, on moonlight nights frequently worked very late. On such occasions Kinjiro was never the first to propose going home, no matter how late it was. Finally, Saburo would say, "Brother, the foxes are howling; let us go home." After some urging, Kinjiro would consent to go. It is thought in Japan that the foxes [1] and badgers do not prowl about until near midnight, and those who hear them think the hour late, and the place lonely.

When Kinjiro was not yet sixteen years of age, his mother took sick, and the whole responsibility of the home was thrown upon him, as well as the added expense of caring for his sick mother, who shortly afterwards breathed her last. When his mother died, they had a family consultation,[2] and decided that the younger brothers should be adopted by one of their relatives and that Kinjiro should go to his uncle, Manbei.

Kinjiro was cared for by his uncle for some time. In return he worked very hard during the day, but spent his nights in study. Manbei, though not

[1] There were superstitions in ancient Japan that foxes and badgers sometimes took the human form in order to bewitch people. The superstition is not entirely dead yet among the illiterate.

[2] It is usual in Japan, when anything is to be decided regarding the welfare of the family or a member of the family, to call all the relatives together for consultation.

1. CULTIVATING THE WASTE LAND IN ORDER TO BUY OIL FOR STUDY.
2. NINOMIYA STUDYING IN SECRET.

STUDENTS AT NINOMIYA'S SHRINE.

rich, was very miserly, and disliked to see the boy wasting oil and time in study, so he decided to put a stop to it. One day he said to Kinjiro: "I have spent much money on you, and all your feeble efforts during the day will not supply your needs, not to mention the oil you waste at night. What good do you think your learning will be to you in the future?" Kinjiro apologized for the waste of the old man's oil, but was none the less determined to obtain an education. Shortly after this conversation, when he was at a loss to know what to do, he found a small tract of deserted land along the river and began to cultivate it. He planted it with young shoots of rice that the farmers had thrown away. In the autumn he was able from the proceeds of the rice to buy oil, and continue his studies. This enraged his uncle, who said to him: "What good is your study to me? If you do not wish to sleep at night, come and help me." Kinjiro obeyed, but from that time he pursued his studies in secret, and rising in the small hours of the morning, read to his heart's content.

Kinjiro was not a selfish boy. Even at this time he is said to have given part of the proceeds of the grain raised by the river to the poor, and to have deposited the balance with the village chief for future use.

CHAPTER II

WHEN Ninomiya was old enough to do for himself, he left his uncle's home, and returned, with the money he had earned, to his father's house. He put the old house in repair, and lived there alone, working hard, and spending as little as possible. The money thus saved was intrusted to a friend, and allowed to accumulate, until, in a remarkably short time, he had completely redeemed his father's estate. Then Ninomiya married.

About this time a certain clansman of the Odawara daimio, named Hattori Jurobei, was in financial trouble. In spite of the fact that he had received the large allowance of 1300 koku (about 6700 bushels) of rice yearly, he was very deeply in debt, and could not get out. In fact, the debt was gradually increasing, and if something were not done to redeem him, he must very soon lose his position. Some one advised him to hire Ninomiya to finance his business. Ninomiya, however, several times refused, but at last, yielding to the importunities of the unfortunate man, he accepted the responsibility. He put his own house under the management of his wife, and entered the home of Hattori, where he was given unconditional control of everything. Under these conditions he agreed to redeem the place in five years. His first step was to give Hattori his orders. He said to him: "You must leave the whole thing to me, and must not even question my actions. You acknowledge your own failure, now you must depend on me to redeem your lost estate. You must not wear silk, and must not have luxury in your home, which must be very simply furnished." In short, he told his master that he must adopt the simple life.

After five years of careful economy and hard work, he paid the debt, and had 300 ryo (about $1500) to the good. When the day came on which he had agreed to report, he went to his master and mistress, and said: "I thank you for your confidence in me, and for the task you have intrusted to me. I have paid your debts, and have 300 ryo left. I offer this money to you as a gift, in recognition of the confidence you have bestowed upon me. One hundred ryo should be put aside for a rainy day, one hundred should be given to my mistress who has so energetically done her duty during this struggle, the balance you may spend as you please." Hattori was delighted, and expressed great admiration for his benefactor, regretting that he had no adequate reward to give him for his services. He then offered Ninomiya the one hundred ryo at his disposal. Ninomiya accepted it, saying, "You are now out of debt, but if you are not careful, you will soon be into debt again." He then advised him to make it a rule to set aside 300 koku of grain yearly, as a safeguard against any emergency that might arise. Ninomiya then bade his master and mistress good-by, went to the servants' room, and divided the money among them, saying : "You have been very faithful servants, I cannot express my admiration for you. Your labor and thrift have saved your master. He gave me this reward. Take it and ever be as you have been, good and faithful." He then went home with no other reward than the consciousness of having done his duty to his fellow-man.

An interesting story is told in connection with this event. Ninomiya observed that a pot took longer to boil when covered with soot, and thus required more charcoal. The servants would not attend to this little detail of economy, and keep the pots clean, so he agreed to buy the soot from them. After that the pots were always shining.

Ninomiya's first marriage was not a happy one. His wife was expecting much money from his work for Hattori, so, when he returned home, she waited expectantly for him to produce his reward; but when it seemed that he was not going to do so, she asked him for it. He told her he was sorry he had nothing for her, and explained how he had distributed the surplus money. She was terribly disappointed, and said it was very disagreeable to be married to such a man. One evening shortly after, she demanded an immediate divorce, on the ground that there was no outlook for the future with a man who cared so little for money. Ninomiya quietly pleaded with her not to be rash. As the days passed, she grew more and more dissatisfied, and again asked for her liberty. Ninomiya now said that, since she was so unhappy, he would let her go, but he would not like her to go penniless. So he asked her to remain until she could earn enough to provide herself with a new outfit of clothes and a little pocket money. She consented to this, and when the time of her departure came, she went off contented and happy. Years after, when Ninomiya had become famous, he visited her native village on business. She wished to see him, but he supposed that she wanted money, for in the meantime she had been married to a very poor man, so he refused to see her, but sent word that, if she wanted money, she might go to a certain place in the road the next morning, and as he passed that way he would drop some money in a paper on the road, and she could pick it up, but he would not give it to her personally. The next morning the wretched woman did as she was directed, and, as he and his train passed by, he did as he had promised. Ninomiya's second wife was a very different woman.

Okubo, the wise and clever lord of Odawara, was delighted when he heard what Ninomiya had done for his retainer, and would like to have taken him into his service at once, but as Ninomiya was a farmer, and therefore considered to be low class, it was difficult to employ him among his samurai. At last a good idea occurred to him. There was a very difficult task that had already been assigned to many officials in turn, but they had all failed to accomplish the work. If Ninomiya were to do this work well, it would be a very easy matter to give him an important place among his retainers.

Utsu, a branch of the Odawara family, lived in Sakuramachi village (not far from Utsunomiya), in Shimotsuke province, where he ruled over a territory that should yield at least 4000 koku [1] of rice, and support about 450 farm-houses. The villagers, however, wasted their time in riotous living and gambling, so that the place only raised about 800 koku, and supported only 150 farm-houses. Besides this, the houses were not kept in repair, and the place was fast becoming a waste.

[1] One koku is almost five bushels.

Ninomiya requested to go to Sakuramachi, by Lord
Odawara's Messenger.

Okubo had made several attempts to improve it, but with little success. He had despatched men and money, but these men became victims to the evil ways of the place, and gave up their task in disgrace. Okubo now turned to Ninomiya for help, but he constantly refused the responsibility. Finally, after three years of importunate entreaty, Ninomiya consented to go and see the place, and study the situation. After visiting the village, he reported that it had been so long neglected, and the people were in such a miserable condition, that it would take much time and labor to reform them. However, he felt certain that, were proper steps taken to stimulate the people to diligence and industry, in time a great work could be successfully accomplished. Okubo asked him about the expense, but Ninomiya said that the previous failures had been largely due to the fact that too much money had already been given. Then he promised that, if the work were assigned to him, not a penny need be paid toward it. Okubo did not understand, and asked for an explanation, saying that he could not see how any great work could be successfully accomplished without money, especially as all the previous efforts had required such large sums. Ninomiya said that the habits of the people degenerated through the misuse of money. They appreciated it because it gave them a chance to gamble, and the more money they had, the more they gambled. They must earn their money to appreciate it. "If you wish to help the wild, you must make the wild help itself." He further explained that were they to cultivate one acre of waste land, and only raise one koku and a half of rice, the people would have none to waste, for one koku would be required for food, and the balance for seed the following year. Such a method of procedure would eventually make them industrious, sober, and economical. He also pointed out that Japanese land had been cultivated, and her industries improved without help from foreign countries, and so in the same way this place must be developed, if it were to be improved at all. Lord Okubo was delighted with the wisdom of his method, and immediately set him to work.

CHAPTER III

NINOMIYA had not accepted this work without counting the cost and laying plans as to his method of procedure. Accordingly, when appointed to do the work, he hastened home, told his wife that he had received a very important commission from Lord Okubo, and that he intended to accomplish it successfully, cost what it would. He said he would do the work, even if he had to die for his master and for the people of the place for which he was about to give so much time and labor. He then gave his wife the choice of going with him, or remaining at home alone, as his first wife had done in the case of the former undertaking. But like every true Japanese wife, she chose to go with him, telling him that a woman once married ought not to return to her parents. "When I left my father's home, I made up my mind to stand by you and help you. Please take me to your battlefields; I will help you fight your battles." This was a great inspiration to Ninomiya, who was often helped and encouraged by the noble, self-sacrificing spirit

89

of his second wife. Ninomiya was just thirty-six years old at this time, and was full of strength and vigor.

When Ninomiya agreed to undertake this work, he rejected the offer of money made by Lord Okubo, on the ground that it was against his principles to run in debt, or to use another's money to do his own work, and besides this, as we have already noted, he thought that the waste places should be made to develop themselves. But he had to have money in order to make a start, so he sold out completely, — house, furniture, implements, and personal belongings, — obtaining thereby about six ryo. There is a record of the assets received from this sale, which in part is as follows : —

One stick for carrying burdens on the shoulders,
sold to Mr. Benzaimon . . . . 280 mon[1]
Five bundles of kindling wood, sold to Mr.
Denzaimon . . . . 72 mon
Two flails for shelling rice, sold to Mr. Jinzo . 180 mon
Four bundles of barley straw, sold to Mr. Ichi-
royemon . . . . 172 mon
Two tubs, sold to So-and-so . . . . . . 312 mon
One kitchen sink, sold to So-and-so . . . . . 200 mon
One old fence at the rear of the house, sold, etc. . 300 mon
One lantern, etc. . . . . 48 mon
Eight bags of rice, etc. . . . .

[1] One mon at that time was equivalent to about one-tenth of a cent to-day.

In this way he has the name of the article, the price, and the buyer carefully recorded in his accounts. He had been the better part of twenty years gathering these things together, but such was his independence of spirit that he sacrificed all for his work and for his lord. Although only a farmer, he had the true spirit of a samurai.

On the morning of his departure, the only one to accompany him, his wife, and their three-year-old child was his brother, Saburo Zayemon, who carried the child as far as Kodzu. There Ninomiya sent him back, thanking him for his trouble. He then put the boy on his own shoulders, and they continued their journey alone.

When Ninomiya arrived at the village about three miles from Sakuramachi, the head of the village and several villagers came out to meet him. Kneeling before him, they welcomed him and invited him to eat and drink with them. But Ninomiya very firmly and politely refused to listen to their request, telling them that his mission was such an important one that he had no time to rest. Thanking them for their kindness, he proceeded on his way to Sakuramachi. These men were not sincere. They were the men who were largely responsible for the condition of affairs at Sakuramachi and the surrounding country. They really meant to flatter Ninomiya, but he was not so easily entrapped, for his quick insight into human nature saved him from their wiles.

Ninomiya went at once to his new home, an old castle that had fallen into disrepair and had become a haunt for foxes and other animals. He began at once to examine the conditions of the people, of which he had received some idea from his former investigations and from the description given him by Lord Okubo. He found that the half had not been told, and that the disorder was really beyond all description. Fully two-thirds of the fields had become waste through neglect; even those around the village that had once been very fertile and productive were now in an uncultivated condition. Poverty had visited the homes, and the people were no longer what they once had been. As the days went by, he discovered that nearly every house in the village was a gambling den or a drinking place. Even the village chiefs were bad men, who sought to enrich themselves at the expense of the villagers. In short, the more he saw of the real conditions, the more formidable did the task of reformation appear.

Nothing daunted, Ninomiya set to work at once, and worked from morning to night among the villagers, going from door to door, and from village to village, helping and encouraging the people. In fine weather and stormy, in cold weather and

warm, Ninomiya was always at work. He praised
the worthy, corrected and taught the unworthy.
He took a very simple meal whenever he ate with
the villagers, refusing all dainties, saying: "Rice
and Miso are good enough for me. I will eat no
dainties till your conditions are improved." He
was accustomed to sit up late into the night plan-
ning his method of procedure for the following
day.

His work, as might be expected, was not without opposition. There were many vicious men
among the villagers, and the worst of these
tried to interfere with his work. The most trouble-
some man was an official who had been sent by the
lord of Odawara to help Ninomiya, although in
reality he had been sent in the hope that Ninomiya's influence would do him good. As is generally the case with such men, they dislike those
who are trying to do them good, so this man hated
Ninomiya, and thwarted as many of his plans as
he could. He even used his own position, as an
official, for this purpose. Sometimes he would
shout at the villagers who were working according
to Ninomiya's command, and order them to cease
working. He would ask them if Ninomiya told
them to do such foolish things, and when they said
he had, this petty official, in the name of the lord
of Odawara, would command them to cease, and

if they disobeyed, he threatened to punish them. The poor people were often at a loss to know what to do, and would sometimes even stop work at the command of this insolent official.

Ninomiya bore those insults patiently, but things went from bad to worse, until finally he concluded it was better to get rid of this man as easily as possible. The official was fond of "sake" (Japanese rice wine) and had several times led the villagers in drunken brawls; knowing this, Ninomiya sent his wife with some "sake" for him. She told him that her husband had sent her with these gifts in recognition of the kind of service he had received from him. She then urged him to rest from his work and drink to his heart's content. The man was very much delighted and remained at home eating and drinking. It sometimes happens that too much of a good thing is bad, but it turned out, in this case, that too much of a bad thing was good for this man, for under his primitive "Gold Cure for Drunkenness" he became a reformed man, and not only became temperate, but ceased to retard the good work Ninomiya was trying to do.

There was a mat maker in the village named Genkichi, who sometimes worked for Ninomiya. He did not work very industriously, and even when he did, he spent all he earned on drink. Once just before the New Year, when others were making their New Year's "mochi" (rice cakes), Genkichi came to Ninomiya to borrow money to make mochi. Ninomiya looked at him a little while, and then said : "You have no right to eat mochi. You have been idling your time and spending your money on drink; how can you expect to eat mochi at New Year's? This season does not come suddenly. There have been 365 days in which to prepare for it. Mochi rice does not spring out of the ground suddenly. It must be sown months before it can be used. Instead of making preparations and sowing rice, you have wasted your time in idleness and your money in wine. You have no right to eat mochi. I will not lend you any money. In future you must be industrious and cease drinking wine. Go to the mountains and gather dead leaves and let them rot for manure. Then rent some land, and sow it, and a year from now you may eat mochi." Genkichi understood his meaning, and turned to go. He walked off with such evident disappointment that, as his dejected figure passed out of the gate, Ninomiya, who had been watching him, called, "Genkichi, Genkichi, come back." Genkichi was surprised to be called back, but returned and stood before Ninomiya, who said, "Do you understand me?" Genkichi said he did. "But are you sure you understand me real well?" Again the reply was that he did. Ninomiya then told him to go to the kitchen and get some mochi rice and some radish. He handed him a little money, telling him he would help him for that year, but the following year he must see to it that he was ready for New Year's. The advice, so strongly and reasonably put, was so effective that the mat maker became a changed man.

CHAPTER IV

SOME OF NINOMIYA'S METHODS

SOME one asked Ninomiya on what principle he acted in his treatment of men, suggesting that they supposed he treated them as if they were his own children. Ninomiya told them that such treatment was not sufficient. "We are related to our children by very strong ties of nature, but in our relation to others we have not those ties to bind us. People who are not related to us come when favor is given, and go when it is withheld, therefore we must love other people twice as much as we do our own children, if we would have them in our land." This gives us some idea of his attitude toward the people of Sakuramachi. At first he began by remitting their taxes and supplying the destitute with food and lodging, but he found that the more he gave, the more they wanted, and the more helpless they became. Ninomiya soon perceived that he was doing harm, and concluded that it was a mistake to give people what they do not earn, or what they are not worthy of receiving. When plants are old, and about to die, no amount of manure can make them thrive, but new plants, carefully and wisely nurtured, grow very quickly. So some men are so fixed in their bad habits that they are almost past redemption. Like old plants they will soon die, and to nurture them is only to hasten their end. He therefore decided to give them the benefit of moral suasion, and leave them alone. He planned to reform the place by bringing in young men, and training them as he desired. Accordingly he took steps to leave the worst of the old men undisturbed, and to use their sons, who like fresh young sprouts quickly responded to his trained touch.

This change of policy was noticed by his enemies, who complained to Lord Okubo that Ninomiya was neglecting the people and letting them go to the bad, without making an effort to save them. Lord Okubo questioned Ninomiya very closely as to his methods, and having satisfied himself that the complaints were without any real justification, he was on the point of punishing the men who had complained, when Ninomiya himself interceded for them and secured their pardon. By this act of generosity his position was strengthened, not only with his master, but also with the people, who lost no time in coming to express their heartfelt thanks. Some of them showed their sincerity by living better lives from that time forward.

Ninomiya's plans had been fairly successful, but the work was very slow. Feeling somewhat discouraged, he decided to appeal to Heaven for help. Some hold that Ninomiya was sincere in this action, and that he really felt his dependence upon some power higher than himself; others held that his action was purely spectacular, that he wished to win the people by an appeal to their religious and superstitious nature. But whatever his motive may have been, he went to the Buddhist temple at Narita to pray for the success of his work. He secured lodging at the inn, and was daily in the attitude of worship before the god, fasting and bathing in cold water. He made several short prayers, and some definite vows before the god. He prayed that calamity, including death, disease, accident, and debt, might be replaced by blessing, prosperity, and happiness. He prayed that deserted wastes and barren soil might give place to well-cultivated plains and rich, productive farm lands; that poverty, tribulation, and hardness might be replaced by wealth and joy, and by all that was for the good of the people. He vowed that he would renounce everything that was detrimental to human development, and that he would endeavor to give them everything that would tend to make their lives truly blessed. He continued thus for twenty-one days. The priest afterward said that he admired Ninomiya's un-selfish spirit. Instead of praying for his own selfish benefit, as others did, he prayed for the people.

Ninomiya had gone to Narita[1] secretly. Not even the officials knew his whereabouts. They became alarmed at his continued absence, and sent a messenger in search of him. The first clew they received was from a messenger of the hotel where Ninomiya was lodging. It seemed that for some reason, after Ninomiya had paid a sum of money in advance, on his lodging account, the landlord became very suspicious of him. He was not re-assured even when told that Ninomiya was a samurai of the Odawara clan, but, pleading that his house was overcrowded, tried to send him away. Ninomiya was indignant, and thundered out: "Why did you not refuse me when I first entered your hotel? Has your house suddenly become full? I have come here to worship at this temple for the good of others. What reason have you to be sus-picious of me? Let your suspicions cease." The

---

[1] Even yet Narita shrine is popular. The God "Fudo Myo" was Ninomiya's favorite. It was a man standing unmoved in the midst of fire with a drawn sword in his right hand to cut out evil and a rope in his left hand to bind it up. The ancient soldier sometimes wore it on his armor as he went to battle. It represents that spirit in the Japanese people that enabled them to defeat the Russian armies every time. Psychologically this idol has had a great place in making Japanese people what they are, strong and courageous.

landlord, frightened, became very humble, and apologized for his conduct. However, he secretly sent a messenger to Odawara to inquire about this strange man, who had come to pray for others. The Odawara men did not know why he had gone to Narita, but they assured the messenger that he was one of their trusted clansmen. After this he was the guest of honor in the little hotel. As soon as the people of Sakuramachi knew where Ninomiya had gone, they gathered together for consultation. They were alarmed lest he intended to desert them, so they decided to send a messenger, urging his return, promising to obey his every word, and to be more diligent in future than they had been in the past. The messenger arrived on the last day of the fast, and as soon as Ninomiya had heard their message, he ate a bowl of rice, and set out for Sakuramachi, running all the way. He arrived there that evening. The people were surprised that, after such a long fast, he was able to run fifty miles. They knew he had been praying for them, and were so impressed by it that they regarded him with the same awe and reverence that they felt toward the gods. From that time Ninomiya's work prospered.

To-day some critics say that while it is true that Ninomiya did a great work for Sakuramachi and the surrounding villages, yet, to appeal to this

Buddhist temple for help, was unworthy of a truly great man. His disciples justify his action by the circumstances which prompted it. Surrounded by jealous officials, who constantly thwarted his plans, he was unable to accomplish his task. Having exhausted all his methods and energy, he felt he must rely on Heaven. They sometimes silence criticism by saying, "Only a sage can understand the heart and spirit of a sage," intimating that, were they as wise as Ninomiya, they would then be in a position to understand and criticise his action and motive.

Ninomiya got up so early, and went to bed so late that it is said his own boys scarcely knew him, and that he did not know just how they had grown. When he was working at Sakuramachi, he used to walk about seven miles to a neighboring village early in the morning, before the people were up, returning after they had retired. He did this for months. When he returned each night, he took his evening meal, taught his disciples, walked around the village, and then retired.

He wrote very many letters every day, employing a secretary. Once he made a mistake in dictating a letter, but when the scribe pointed it out he refused to have it rewritten, saying that if the scribe corrected it, then the writing would be the scribe's, and not his own.

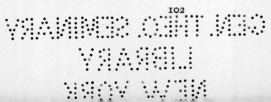

One morning he went to the laborers' shanty and found the men standing around doing nothing. He asked why they were not at work, and received the reply that they were waiting for the water to boil, as they could not eat cold rice. Ninomiya, very much annoyed, said: " Your village is in a dilapidated condition. If your spirit is such that you can hang around this shanty until this hour of the day waiting for water to boil, you can never hope to restore it to prosperity." So saying, he took the kettle and emptied its contents on the ground, bidding them eat their rice cold and get to work.

Ninomiya said: "It is natural for a man to try to hide the fact that he is in debt, and so the debt gradually increases. To remedy this, if you are in debt, you must paste up the amount of your debt in front of the god shelf, so that every day when you worship at the family altar, you will see it. In this way your debt will in time be wiped out."

Once he met the chief of " one hundred and four gamblers." [1] The gambler's wife dressed very gayly,

[1] I was told that the city in which we lived was divided into sections for gambling called "Nawa-Bari" (rope boundaries). Over each section there was a recognized chief who received a percentage on all gambling done within his district. Some of these men were little demigods. I heard of one of them who refused to pay rent for the house he had seen fit to occupy. The landlord, fearing his influence, left him in possession until the covering of the mats became so worn that he vacated the house of his own accord. Some of them are wealthy. The best house

and spent her time in idleness. Ninomiya desired to reform the man, and planned an object lesson for him. He went to this man's wife and asked her to spin some yarn, but she refused, on the ground that she was not poor, and did not need to work. But Ninomiya petitioned her so humbly, offering her double pay, that she finally consented to do the work. She worked until he was able to put fifty yen in her hand. The gambler was struck by Ninomiya's action, and inquired into the cause of it. He concluded that the reason was not hard to find; the sage wanted to show him that money could be earned little by little in an honest way. Under the influence of his wife, he became a good and useful citizen.

There was a gambler in Aoki village very much opposed to Ninomiya, who was really at a loss to know what to do with him. One day an incident occurred that gave Ninomiya his golden opportunity to win him. Ninomiya's servant, when on an errand, had rushed into this man's outhouse with such force that, to his chagrin, the rotten

in our street belonged to one of these men. When he died, we were requested by the head man of the street for a cent as a slight indication of sympathy for the family. We acceded to the request, and to our surprise that evening we received a magnificent Japanese feast which a servant brought to our door. On the day of the funeral, when his body was being carried to the crematory, men went before the procession scattering small coins for the bystanders to pick up.

NINOMIYA REPAIRING THE GAMBLER'S GATE.

building gave way and fell to the ground. The gambler was very angry, and chased the servant right into the office of the sage, who, rising, calmly asked the man what had occurred to make him so angry. On hearing the man's complaint, Ninomiya replied that the building could not have been in a very good state of repair, if his servant could thus accidentally destroy it. He supposed that the man's residence was also in need of repairs. The man excused himself on the ground of poverty. A few days after this, Ninomiya sent men and built new buildings for the man. Thus by the art of love this gambler was won from his evil ways, and became one of Ninomiya's right-hand supporters.

One year, during the Tempo Era (1830–1844 A.D.), Ninomiya went out in the beginning of summer to see the crops. He tasted an egg plant and was surprised to find that already it tasted as it should in autumn. As the weather continued bad, he called all the farmers together, and told them that he feared a famine. He ordered them to dig up a part of their fields, and sow millet [1] instead of rice, as he feared that the rice would not mature. They followed his advice, and when the harvest came there was no rice, but the millet was abundant. In this way they were saved from

[1] Millet is grown in poor places and eaten by the poor instead of rice.

the distress of famine by the remarkable foresight of Ninomiya.

Ninomiya once said: "We have to vary our method of procedure to suit different circumstances. For example, if a farmer is sick and unable to work, and you go to help him, you would naturally start with the most neglected parts of the farm, but in doing so you are foolish. First clean the bad weeds out of the best fields, then if you have not time to do more, leave the worst fields as they are. Otherwise you will not leave any one place in proper condition. Again, if when you are cultivating a mountain field, you come to a root of a large tree, do not waste time digging it out, but cultivate around it for two or three years, and it will naturally rot away. And when you are trying to reform a deserted place, pay no attention to opposition, but go quietly about your work, and make it succeed. In the end the opposition will melt away. This teaching is very important for human life."

CHAPTER V

THERE was a barren tract of land about a mile square in one of the villages. To put this under cultivation many men were employed from other districts to assist the villagers. Ninomiya was very busy supervising them. In the morning he was there when the laborers came, and lost no time in getting them to work. At sunset he was the last to leave. His orders were so kindly given, and so effectually acted upon, that fifty men were able to do about as much work as one hundred would under ordinary circumstances. Ninomiya knew his men, and could administer words of blame or praise very effectively. In a few months the work was completed to his satisfaction.

Among the workmen there was one who seemed to be very diligent. Two or three of the bosses commended him for his work, and admired him for his industry. They expected that Ninomiya would praise him, and were surprised that he did not. One day Ninomiya scolded him very severely in the presence of the other men, saying: "You cunning fellow, you deceitful shirk, do you expect to deceive us by your shallow tricks? You pretend to be very diligent when we are beside you, but when our backs are turned, you are idle and lazy. Do you think you can work at your present rate all day? If you were to try for just one day, you would break yourself down. Try it and see." The man was very much ashamed of being detected in this way, and bowed to the ground, saying nothing, but Ninomiya continued: "Such a deceitful man as you are would soon contaminate the rest of the men. Go, and never show your face around here again. Go." The man was so humbled, and begged so earnestly for pardon, that Ninomiya relented, and pardoned him.

There was another man about sixty years old, who was very diligent digging up the roots of trees. The poor old man refused to rest when others did, saying, "You young men can work hard when you work, but I cannot do as much as you can in the same time, so I must work while you rest." One of the bosses found fault with him, and said: "The old man is only digging up roots from day to day. He is not worth even a third as much as one of the others, but Ninomiya does not find fault with him or his work." One day Ninomiya called the old man and asked him where he lived. He replied that he was from a village in Kasamo province, and belonged to a very poor

THE INDUSTRIOUS OLD MAN.

family.   His family of boys were now grown up and
farming for themselves.   He was not needed at
home any longer, and rather than be a burden on his
sons, he thought he could help relieve the poverty
of his home by going out to work.   He then thanked
Ninomiya for his lenient attitude toward him,
in permitting him to work at the same wage, along
with much younger men.   Ninomiya offered him a
large sum of money in recognition of his earnest
work.   The old man's face changed color at Ninomiya's words of commendation, but he very
politely refused to accept the gift, saying it was
sufficient that he, an old man, should receive the
same salary as the young men.   In fact, he felt
that he had already received more than he earned,
and why should he accept any further reward?
Ninomiya told him that he had been watching him
for several months, and had admired his spirit
very much, especially as he had noticed that he
worked just as hard when the boss was absent, as
when he was present.   He also noticed that he did
not rest when others did, and had chosen the work
most men avoided, viz. pulling up roots.   He then
urged him to accept the money, for his influence
and example had been a very great help in performing this important work.   He said further: "You
say you are poor, but I say that in the spirit you
manifest in your work, and in your persistent refusal

of money you feel you have not earned, you are rich. This money is really not my reward to you, it is in fact the reward of Heaven for faithful service. We are apt to see only the things you mention, but Heaven looks at your heart, and rewards accordingly." These unexpected words of praise almost broke the old man down, and bowing very low, he accepted the gift of Heaven, with evident gratitude and pleasure. One of Ninomiya's striking traits was that he was quick to see faithful service, and to reward it.

Once when Ninomiya was on a tour of inspection around a certain village, he and his companion came to a dirty, neglected house in which there lived some idle people. Ninomiya told the owner that if he did not desire the presence of the god of poverty in his home, he had better clean it all up, and pull up the weeds and grass in the garden. Moreover, the god of poverty would be accompanied by the god of disease, unless he cleaned up the place. "In filth, unclean flies swarm; in grass and bad weeds, snakes and reptiles live; in unclean flesh, worms gather; in corrupt water, wigglers accumulate; and in the impure soul, sin and crime are rampant." As he passed on, he came to a small house, clean inside and out. He remarked that a gambler probably lived there, because, although the house was clean, there were no farm implements or other indications of industry to be seen. This man, he said, was a sinner among farmers. The men with him were struck by his keen insight.

Ninomiya said he could tell a man's character, to some extent at least, even from one sentence he might hear him speak. If he heard a man say, "In Yedo, one has to buy water," he concluded that the man was lazy, but if he heard him say, "In Yedo, even by selling water, a man can make money," he concluded that man was industrious. If he heard a man say in the evening about nine o'clock, "It is about ten o'clock," he concluded that man was inclined to be indolent. If he said, "Oh, it is not yet much after nine o'clock," he decided he was industrious. In this way we can estimate a man's spirit from what he says.

CHAPTER VI

NINOMIYA AND YENNO THE PRIEST

THE estate of Karasuyama, under Lord Okubo, in the same province as Sakuramachi village, gradually became desolate because of the idle and immoral habits of the people. Year after year the population and the crops decreased. The lord of the place and his officials did not know how to remedy the trouble, for, in spite of all they did, the place went from bad to worse.

Yenno, a priest of Tenshoji, a temple belonging to Lord Okubo, was a straightforward man, somewhat learned. He pitied the people very much, giving them money to help them in their distress. He even introduced laborers to help them cultivate their fields, but it was of no avail. Nature seemed to work against the benevolence of the priest, for just at that time a great famine broke over the district, leaving the poor people in a worse state than ever, and more than counteracting all he had done to help them.

By this time the work of Ninomiya was becoming famous, and hearing of it, Yenno urged Sugenoya, the chief minister of the estate, to accompany him

YENNO THE PRIEST AT NINOMIYA'S GATE.

to consult the sage, as to the best means of relieving the distress of the people. Sugenoya refused to go, but gladly gave his consent to the priest going. Yenno went to Sakuramachi village, and sought an interview with Ninomiya, who refused to be interviewed, saying: "Priests should do what they are taught to do by Buddha. As for me I have my own work to do and cannot leave it, even for a moment, to talk to an idle monk." Yenno was not to be put off in this way, and refused to leave the place until he should see the sage. He said: "True I am a priest, but I have come to the great teacher, to be taught how to relieve the people who are dying. I cannot and will not return until I am taught." He again requested Ninomiya to hear him, but Ninomiya replied: "The lord of the place is responsible for the good of the people of Karasu-yama. You officious monk, what business is it of yours?" Yenno was disappointed, but still refused to go. He seated himself on the sod in front of the gate, saying: "The life of the people hangs upon my success. I will not return until I get the needed instruction. No, not even if I die. I prefer to starve myself, rather than see the death of my people." So he remained there until he was wet with dew, and faint with hunger. In the morning, the servants were surprised to see him still there, and they reported it to their master, who called out in a loud and irritable manner: "What a persistent monk! Bring him to me." Then Yenno was brought before Ninomiya, who in an excited manner told him: "The fault lies with yourself. Every man has his respective calling. The lord must superintend his people, and the people must faithfully obey their lord. Even the priest must perform his own duties. If the priest tries to do the work of the lord, and the lord tries to do the work of the retainer, naturally there will be great disturbance in the province. You, a priest, are trying to usurp your lord's position. You are trying to cultivate barren wastes, and relieve the distress of the people. Such work is the responsibility of your lord. You should be at the temple teaching the people. Your purpose is good, but your methods are bad. Why did you not prefer dying in your temple, to dying like a beggar at our gate? You are neglecting your duty, and your lord is neglecting his, and the people are suffering because of your mistakes. Return to your temple, and to your own calling." Yenno understood and hurried back to tell the chief minister what he had heard.

Ninomiya's treatment of Yenno may have been due to the fact that he did not like Buddhist priests and scholars. He was once asked his reason for this, and he replied that he did not like those who were mere consumers, and not producers; men who were receiving their "botamochi"[1] from another's, and not from their own, labor. He did not like a plagiarist, because he used another's work as if it were his own. He urged his own disciples not to teach what they had merely heard, but to first make it their own and manifest it in their characters and lives. His attitude toward Yenno may be partly explained by his attitude to priests in general, and partly by his custom of refusing to be interviewed by those who had not convinced him of their sincerity.

Sugenoya was pleased with what he heard from Yenno, and at once set out to report it to his lord, and to get an introduction to Ninomiya. He then hurried to Sakuramachi for further light on the subject. Ninomiya said: "I am sorry that I am not in a position to help you, but the fact is that after several years' toil here, in the service of my lord, there is little to show for it. But if my lord bids me work for your estate, I shall be glad to do what I can to help you. Fortunately our lords are relatives, and that makes it easy for me to undertake work for your lord. It will take a long time to see much fruit for our toil, so I will give you this 100 ryo to help tide you over."

---

[1] Botamochi is a very sweet ball of broiled glutinous rice, rolled in a composition of beans and sugar.

Sugenoya was delighted to receive so much money in such a time of distress, but he was somewhat surprised at Ninomiya's spirit, and returned home in a very thoughtful mood.

The people of Karasuyama were at the mercy of the many famines that occurred during these times. They often had to eat roots and grass. At such times many riots took place in the district, for the distressed people attacked the homes of the wealthy, and stole rice and other eatables. The rich, in turn, fortified their homes, and kept a strong guard ready to defend their goods against such attacks. During one of these famines, when the country was at its worst, Lord Okubo ordered the people of Sakuramachi village to help the people of Karasuyama as much as possible. Ninomiya immediately sent them rice valued at about 2000 ryo, as well as other provisions. The procession that took the food was over twenty miles long. Eleven storehouses, which resembled the storehouses of Joseph, were built in the enclosure of Yenno's temple, and rice gruel was given out to the people. The good Yenno himself worked from morning until night at this work that he was largely responsible for initiating. It was a strong evidence of the success of Ninomiya that while other places were in want, his once deserted and poverty-stricken villages were supplied with

YENNO FEEDING THE FAMINE SUFFERERS.

enough and to spare. Soon after this, the people of Karasuyama, under his direction, became diligent and thrifty. In two or three years they had several hundred acres of land under cultivation, and were able to lay aside several hundred bushels of rice every year against such famines as had previously distressed the people.

CHAPTER VII

NINOMIYA'S ATTITUDE TOWARD THE SPIRIT OF REVENGE

NEAR the Ryogoku bridge in Yedo a man avenged the death of his father. His valor and filial piety were praised by all who heard of it. Ninomiya, hearing one of his disciples praising him, said: "It is not good to praise the avenger. Iyeyasu,[1] being born in a warlike age, admired revenge in his youth. But Yuyo, a famous Buddhist priest, taught him that revenge was not good, and that if he wished to rule the country well he must be benevolent. He must see that revenge is inhuman. Iyeyasu was so influenced that he discountenanced revenge from that time forth. This teaching applies to all the people in Japan. We must cherish benevolence, and do away with

[1] In a work called "The Legacy of Iyeyasu," Chapter XV, Iyeyasu is quoted as saying: "In my youth my sole aim was to conquer and subjugate inimical provinces and to take revenge upon the enemies of my ancestors. Yuyo teaches, however, that 'to assist the people is to give peace to the Empire,' and since I have come to understand that the precept is founded on sound principle, I have unhesitatingly followed it. Let my posterity follow the principle. Any one turning back on it is no descendant of mine. The people are the foundation of the Empire."

the spirit and custom of revenge. Revenge leads to revenge without limit. If it be encouraged, the world will become a scene of bloodshed and murder. Truly, it is both foolish and inhuman. Every man should not be his own judge, but justice should be carefully administered by the government. If occasion for revenge arises, the government should take the case in hand and administer suitable punishment." The story of Kawasaki Magoyemon will give further light on Ninomiya's attitude toward the spirit of revenge.

Kawasaki Magoyemon, a dealer in cereals, lived in Oiso. He was rich and exceedingly miserly. When the famine we have already spoken of broke out, the people of his district were in such distress that all the rich men who were at all liberal opened their purses and stores, and gave what they could to help the poor. But Magoyemon would give nothing. On the contrary, he went all the way to Yedo to get a higher price for his rice, but to his credit be it said, this enabled him to lower the price of other cereals, and thus appease, to some extent, the anger of the suffering people. But one day when he was away on one of his trips, the starving people gathered around his house and urged the clerks to give them food. They refused to do so, because their master was absent. This was too much for the poor people. A raging mob gathered around the place, and before they dispersed, destroyed the house, divided its contents, and with a great shout of triumph, disappeared. Magoyemon's wife and children were so alarmed that they all ran away.

On his return, Magoyemon was very angry, and set about to get even with his opponents. It is hard to say what evil he might have done, had not the authorities heard of the disturbance, and come to investigate the matter. They reprimanded the people, but as Magoyemon had already done more or less damage, they put him in prison in order to keep the peace. Troubles scarcely ever come singly. While this wretched man was in prison, his wife and family were in great distress. A fire broke out in the town, and burned what the mob had left of his house. His wife took sick, and, gradually sinking under the difficulties that pressed upon her, died, leaving two little children unprovided for. When Magoyemon heard this, he became frantic and paced the floor of his cell like a caged tiger, swearing vengeance on the people, whom he blamed for all his troubles. As a result of his threats, he was still further detained in prison about three years.

Sobei, a brother-in-law of Magoyemon, was very much grieved at the distress of the Kawasaki family, and decided to do all in his power to help

MAGOYEMON IN PRISON.

them. He was one of Ninomiya's disciples, and so he turned to him for advice, telling him all the details of the trouble. When Ninomiya heard the story, he said: "One never raises egg plants from cucumber vines. Such great distress must have a natural cause. If the family do not know the cause, it has probably taken such root that no human effort can extract it." So saying, he sighed, and remained silent, but Sobei, not yet satisfied, urged him to continue. He then said: "It is impossible to relieve the family unless Magoyemon repents, and turns over a new leaf. Heaven renders good for good, and bad for bad. Your wife, as sister of Magoyemon, must take measures to save his home, or it will be destroyed. If she desires to help her brother, she must show her sympathy for him, and practise such economy that she will be able to help him in a material way. Tell her to take back the things she received from her father's home. If she does so, her brother's heart will be touched, he will be converted, and the former happiness will be restored to the family. Time may cause even the tiniest seed to become a great tree, spreading its branches in the air. The true human heart may move even Heaven." Sobei was delighted, and immediately he and his wife put these instructions into practice. His brother, Yoshisuke, went to the prison and reported to Magoyemon the teaching of Ninomiya, and the action of his sister. He was touched to the heart, and seemed ashamed of his past spirit and conduct. His better nature gradually asserted itself, and his bitter spirit towards his enemies by degrees relaxed; when the authorities saw the change, they set him free.

When Magoyemon found his motherless children in such a miserable condition, and heard the complaints of his former steward, his old spirit of hatred and revenge began to return. He went to his dead wife's home, and secretly consulted with her relatives as to the best means of restoring his fallen fortunes, and of avenging his enemies. Sobei was very grieved when he heard of this meeting, and advised his brother-in-law to visit Ninomiya. To induce him to go, he said that he thought Ninomiya would be willing to lend him at least one thousand ryo, without interest. Magoyemon and his father-in-law did not believe Sobei, but under the circumstances they were willing to see what could be done. At this time Ninomiya was visiting the head of Takematsu village, so they called there and asked to see him. He was in the bath and overheard them at the door. Feeling that Magoyemon was a hopeless case, he hastily dressed, and slipping out the back door ran about six miles to a farmhouse, where he was known. His host, and the guests, began to think that Ninomiya was a long time in the bath, so they went to the bathroom, but found it empty. They then inquired for him in the village, but he was nowhere to be found, so they concluded that his sudden departure was due to the visit of Magoyemon.

The following morning, messengers were sent everywhere in search of Ninomiya. When they finally discovered him, the village chief and the three guests urged him to return, but he refused, and remained in the farm-house four or five days longer. Sobei and his friends were now very anxious to see him, and to ask for advice and help. Finally yielding to their importunity, he bade them not to interrupt him in his work, for which he was responsible to his lord. This gruff reply silenced all of them except Sobei, who, after bowing politely, urged Ninomiya to suggest some method of restoring Magoyemon's fortunes. Ninomiya said: "Magoyemon seems to be envious of others, without due consideration of his own faults. He is much inferior to his sister, who so wisely followed my advice. His heart craves vengeance on the poor people. He and I are going in opposite directions, for I am ever longing for the good of the people. His path leads to sure self-destruction; he certainly deserves to perish with the devil he carries in his breast." Magoyemon, hearing this from so great a teacher, was convinced of his error

and asked for further directions. His evident earnestness impressed Ninomiya, who continued: "Every effect has a cause. Your distress has been caused by your own malicious spirit, and you are foolish enough to be angry when you find cucumbers growing on cucumber vines. You try to lay your misfortune on the evil disposition of the people, instead of on your own, where it belongs. You ask me to help you obtain a method of restoring your fortunes. It cannot be done unless you see your own faults and mend them. Besides this, you must respect Heaven. You must share your blessings with other people, and help them bear their burdens. If you do this, you are sure to retrieve your lost fortunes." The more Magoyemon heard, the more he wanted to hear, and the more willing he was to mend his ways. Ninomiya, seeing this, continued: "Magoyemon, you probably have something left after your disasters, for you were a very rich man. How much can you gather together from the ruins?" On being told that he could gather about 500 ryo, Ninomiya advised him to get rid of that money also, because he had earned it in a wrong way. Ninomiya, noticing that Magoyemon hesitated, said: "Virtuous men will follow my words, but bad men will not. I do not mean for you to burn the money, or throw it away; I mean for you to give it to the poor and the dis-

MAGOYEMON'S FAMILY.

tressed. You have your business left, and if you persevere in a good way, you will certainly become prosperous. If such a method does not restore your fortunes, and fails to relieve you of the people's envy, I will give you back the money out of my own funds. Go home and do as I have advised." The three left the house and returned home. After many temptations to the contrary, Magoyemon decided to follow the advice he had received. The result was all that Ninomiya had anticipated.

CHAPTER VIII

NAKAMURA GENJIN, a physician in the employ of Lord Hosokawa, another branch of the Okubo family, was a very fine, clever-looking man, but so careless in the management of his household affairs that he fell into debt. The debt gradually increased until it amounted to about twenty-five ryo which, for a man in his position, was large. He was greatly troubled about it, but, hearing that Ninomiya would lend money without interest, he started to Yedo to see him. On being introduced to Ninomiya, he was so anxious to get the money that he began at once to make the request. This so annoyed Ninomiya that he replied in an excited voice: "Self-interest alone has brought you here, for you have never mentioned your lord's welfare. I am ashamed to be seen talking to you. Go from my presence at once, and never darken my door again." Genjin was so completely embarrassed that he could not reply; but, finally regaining his self-possession, he apologized for his mistake, and returned home quite chagrined.

Lord Hosokawa was sixty years old, and child-less, so he adopted Lord Arima's son, Tatsujiro, as his heir. Tatsujiro was very clever and kind-hearted, and was much grieved that his subjects were so distressed by poverty, so he asked Genjin how he could relieve their oppression. Genjin recommended Ninomiya as the only man who could give him much assistance, telling him of the great work at Sakuramachi.

Accordingly Genjin was sent to consult Nino-miya. He gave him a detailed account of the circumstances, and asked his advice as to the best means of relieving the distress. When he heard the appeal, Ninomiya ordered Genjin to bring the account books. After a close and lengthy examination of them, Ninomiya gave Genjin a series of instructions about finances and taxes. Upon examining these instructions, Tatsujiro was delighted with their system and accuracy, and decided to employ Ninomiya. As Ninomiya was too busy to undertake the work, he recommended one of his most reliable disciples, named Oshima, who proved a capable substitute.

During the famine of the seventh year of Tempo Era (1836 A.D.) there were several villages in Suruga province at the foot of Mount Fuji completely without provisions. In Tokyo, Ninomiya met Lord Okubo, who ordered him to go to Odawara, and, having received rice and money, proceed with it to their relief. He gladly undertook the task, and, after travelling day and night, he arrived at Oda-wara, and delivered his message to the chief officials. These men spent the whole morning in consulta-tion. At noon when they proposed to adjourn until they had eaten their midday meal, Nino-miya became very indignant, and reminded them that while they were delaying, thousands were starving. He himself had travelled, without sleep, day and night, so as not to delay relief, but they were not willing to go without even one meal in order to hasten the work. In his opinion they should not eat until they had settled this im-portant matter. They admitted their selfish mistake, and continued in consultation, without interruption, until a decision was reached, and Ninomiya was started on his way with means of relief.

This same famine so affected the people of Oda-wara district that they were forced to eat grass and roots. Conditions became so serious that Lord Okubo sent for Ninomiya to come at once. Ninomiya, however, declined to go, saying: "I am busy relieving the famine sufferers here. Why does his lordship call me at such a time; if he wishes to consult me, he will have to come himself." The messenger became very angry, but reported the answer to his lord, who immediately sent another messenger apologizing for his shortsightedness, and requesting that as soon as Ninomiya could arrange it, he would come to his help. This Ninomiya promised to do.

When the messenger returned, Lord Okubo called his officials to him, and announced his intention of promoting Ninomiya to a high place among his clansmen, in recognition of his great work at Sakuramachi. When Ninomiya arrived, his lordship was very ill, but was anxiously awaiting his coming. No sooner had he arrived than he was presented with a magnificent ceremonial robe, indicating his promotion. When he received it, he said: "How can I afford to dress in such a fine robe at such a critical time as the present? Our people are dying of starvation, and I am called here to help them. I do not wish for robes; I desire provisions of grain and rice to distribute among the people. This rich robe will not help the people; please return it to his lordship." Again Lord Okubo acknowledged his fault, and wished to appoint him to a government position, but Ninomiya refused the honor. His persistent refusal of honors called forth the greatest admiration of the lord of Odawara, who at once took steps to hand over to Ninomiya one thousand ryo, and all the rice and food stored in the castle.

The sick man was pleased that Ninomiya was attached to his person, and, although he had appointed him to superintend the relief work, his chief retainer hesitated to carry out the order, on the ground that no order had been received from Yedo, the seat of the Tokugawa government. Ninomiya said: "The people are starving. His lordship has given orders to help them. You heartless fellows, why do you not open up the stores at once? Delay now is fatal. You ought to be willing to suffer capital punishment if need be, in order to help the people. You stand in hesitation and doubt while the people are dying." His manner and arguments were so effective that they quietly handed him over the stores to distribute. While he was engaged in this work, Lord Okubo died. Ninomiya was deeply grieved when he heard the news, and said, "For ten years I have worked for Lord Okubo, but now he is gone; from whom shall I receive my orders?" He finished the work of relief, helping over 40,000 persons.

Lord Okubo was so closely connected with the work Ninomiya had done that a short account of his life may be interesting, as throwing some light on the formative elements in Ninomiya's ideal. He was born in the first year of Tenmei (1780) in December. At sixteen years of age he succeeded to his father's estates, and at thirty he was ap-

pointed to take charge of the Osaka Castle for the
Tokugawa government. When he was thirty-five,
he was minister for the Shogun in Kyoto, and at
thirty-eight he became minister of state for the
Tokugawa government. From his youth he was
very charitable and benevolent. His ideal was to
build up a noble character. When he was fifteen
years old, he wrote out fifteen articles for the direction of his daily life and conduct. His pure
character in public life and his persistent refusal to
accept bribes were very admirable. Matsudaira[1]
Sadanobu was his ideal of a statesman. Lord
Okubo wore cotton clothes and ate plain food, thus
setting an example of the simple life for others to
follow. After helping the poor in his community,
he put aside the surplus of his income in the "Ten-
shukaku,"[2] a tower built within the castle for religious purposes. When dying, he handed over
10,000 ryo from this surplus fund.

When he was in Kyoto, he received many favors
from H. I. Majesty, the Emperor of Japan, and
was frequently admitted into the imperial gardens.
On one of these occasions the Emperor gave him
his own ink stone. To show his appreciation for

[1] Cf. Introduction.
[2] "Tenshu" means literally "lord of heaven." Some say that this
part of that old castle originated at the time of the first introduction of Christianity into Japan. The Roman Catholic Church is
called the "Tenshukyo."

this gift, he wrote a couple of sayings, one of which expresses his pleasure that he had received that which no one could get, the great ink stone in which the Emperor's pen had been dipped morning and evening. The other says, "Our Emperor's grace gradually drops like dew, becoming a great ocean [1] in this ink stone." When he was forty-three years old, he first employed Ninomiya. He died in the eighth year of Tempo Era, at the age of fifty-seven.

After the death of Lord Okubo, his successor discontinued the method of Ninomiya throughout the estates. Hearing this, many friends came to console with Ninomiya. On one occasion some of these presented him with some potatoes [2] as a gift, and expressed their regret at the opposition that had been offered to his views. Ninomiya said: "My method is just like this potato, it is very easily affected by the weather. Even though it is very delicious and nutritious, it needs care in order to be its best. Bad weeds, in order to thrive, need no such care and protection as this potato. So my method, in order to produce the best results, needs protection." He told his friends to wait patiently and confidently, for in time his method would

[1] This is only appreciated when we know that the depression in the ink stone is the same word as the word for ocean.

[2] Potatoes, eggs, tea, oranges, apples, and other produce are common gifts.

justify itself, and again become popular. There is a story that Ninomiya felt the rejection of his method so keenly that he went to the shrine of the dead man who had been so much to him in life, and told his spirit all about his trouble.

In the thirteenth year of Tempo, in October (1842 A.D.), Ninomiya became an official of the Tokugawa government, and was ordered to construct a canal from the marsh lake Teganuma to Lake Imbra, and from there to the ocean, making this canal a branch of the Tone River. This was done partly for commercial and trade purposes, and partly for the improvement of the conditions of the people. Ninomiya willingly undertook the task, and made a survey of the district. The results of his investigations were written in two Japanese volumes, and presented to the government. For some reason the work was never completed, but the report of Ninomiya is still of value. He advocated a reformation of the ethical and moral conditions of the people as of more importance than the mere improvement of their physical environment. He reported that the people were idle and demoralized, and that without improvement of their spiritual condition it would be impossible to employ them in any government job, for they would idle away their time and waste much valuable money. Even were the country around Lake Imbra properly drained, and even should that district become wealthy, and the conditions greatly improved, the moral standard of the people was such that wealth would only increase the vice and sensuality, already too prominent among them. First improve their moral natures, and then wealth would be a blessing to them instead of a curse.

CHAPTER IX

IKEDA NAOTANE, the chief councillor of Lord Soma, wished to meet Ninomiya, but was again and again refused an audience. Finally, by the assistance of Kusano, a fellow-clansman, who knew Ninomiya, he gained admittance to the presence of the sage, and presented his difficulty. "My master," said he, "is lord of Soma. For several reasons his estate has fallen into poverty. In ancient times it was very prosperous, but by making beautiful gardens and parks and other places of amusement, the people became luxurious and easy-going and the treasury of the estate gradually became empty. To add to our distress, the great famine of Tenmei Era forced us to run into debt to the large sum of 300,000 ryo. The people have become degenerate and demoralized, and the deserted fields have become a resort for badgers and foxes. My master is troubled. We must redeem his estates. After thirty years of effort we are no better off than when we began. In fact, the fields are worse now than they ever were. To add to our distress the famines of the second and seventh years of Tempo Era (1831, 1836) left us without even rice to eat. We had to send to Akita and Osaka for supplies. Your reputation has gone abroad because you have helped several nobles who were in similar circumstances. Please condescend to help my master also." This consultation took place in the thirteenth year of Tempo Era (1842 A.D.).

Ninomiya replied that he was glad to hear that Lord Soma was benovolent, and his subjects loyal, but sorry that, in spite of these excellent qualities, they had failed to remedy the financial situation. He thought their failure was due to the lack of a guiding principle, and suggested that they should adopt the principle of the "Hotoku" society, known as "Bundo," [1] which required that they should so live within their income that they would have a yearly surplus. He offered to examine the books of the estate, and from them to strike an average income. Having obtained this, they must limit the expenditure allowed Lord Soma and his retainers. If they agreed to live within this fixed limit, they would have a yearly surplus which might be used in developing the estate, paying off the debt, or guarding against any emergency that might arise. He pointed out that most of the feudal lords of the time were living beyond their

[1] Almost equivalent to the English word "thrift."

136

means, and were not prepared for possible emergencies.

"If you adopt the method of 'Bundo,' you will be able to meet the demands of Heaven, and your surplus will continue to accumulate. As the water of a great river is not exhausted by those who draw from it, so, acting on this principle, your resources will never be exhausted. Your present method is like a man dipping water from a tub; sooner or later the supply will run out. Japan was once called 'Toyoashiwara,' a great reed-growing plain, but from the time of the first Emperor, Jimmu, its resources have gradually developed without any outlay of money. It has reached its present state of cultivation without borrowing money from foreign countries. It has been developed gradually, spadeful [1] by spadeful, until now almost all Japan has been brought under cultivation." Ninomiya was very much opposed to borrowing money. He believed that if the best possible use were made of the resources at hand, wealth would eventually be accumulated.

Ikeda was delighted with what Ninomiya had taught him, and told his master what he had heard. Lord Soma was also pleased, and in the first year of Kokka (1844 A.D.) invited Ninomiya to take full

[1] There is a principle in the society of "Hotoku" called the "One-spade-full" principle.

charge of his estate. Ninomiya, however, being in the employ of the government, refused the offer, but the government, in sympathy for Lord Soma, granted Ninomiya permission to undertake this work. At the request of the sage, Lord Soma placed in his hands the records of the estate for the past one hundred and eighty years, from the fifth year of Kanbun (1665 A.D.) to the first year of Kokka (1844 A.D.). Ninomiya was pleased to get accurate accounts for so long a period. He said that in most cases it was very difficult to get a systematic account of the receipts for even ten or twenty years. He studied these accounts day and night, and finally made the following interesting classification of his conclusions. In the first period, designated "Heaven," the average yearly income was 140,079 hyo[1] of rice. In the second period, designated "Man," the income was 118,064 hyo of rice per annum, and the third period, designated "Earth," the average was only 63,793 hyo. He averaged these three and got what he called the permanent yearly income of Lord Soma. Next, he took the original figures, and, instead of dividing them into three, he divided them into two periods, designated "The Prosperous Age" and "The Age of Decay." He took the average

[1] One hyo is a straw bag of rice containing half a koku, or about two bushels of grain.

income for the last ten years of the Age of Decay, and made it the standard of expenditure for the period during which he would be redeeming the estate. This standard was to increase every ten years, and he estimated that in sixty years the average would be about 170,000 hyo, or an amount much higher than that reached during the "Heaven" period. He called the "Heaven" period the climax of prosperity, and the "Earth" period, the anticlimax. This examination of the Soma accounts is recorded in three Japanese volumes, and is known as "Iseikwan." [1] Although it is customary for Japanese to designate three volumes of a book as "Heaven," "Earth," and "Man" (ten, chi, jin), Ninomiya changed the usual order, and made "Earth" stand for the worst period. His order of designation is significant, and might imply that man's prosperity depends on man's attitude to "Heaven."

Having decided to employ Ninomiya, Lord Soma, who was residing in Yedo, sent Ikeda to Nakamura, the district he wished to revive first, to consult with the officials, and decide upon the best mode of procedure. When Ikeda arrived, he told them he wished to adopt the method of Ninomiya, who was a teacher worth listening to. He said: "If the method does not succeed, it will be because we are unable to follow Ninomiya's advice. Nino-

[1] "Kwan" means mirror, and "Isei," method of government.

miya's method is not to hurry. If we wish to succeed, we must undertake the work very deliberately. One shovelful after another, in slow but sure succession, will accomplish wonders. One village after another, patiently and carefully developed, will in time reform any number of places." He asked them to choose any village they wished, and they would give Ninomiya's method a trial. They chose the village of Kusano. It was situated between very high mountains, and even in summer was not warm enough for successful farming. The people were very poor, and about every three years were visited by a famine. The retainers thought that if Ninomiya's method would succeed in this village, it would succeed anywhere. When their decision was reported to Ninomiya, he said they did not understand his method, which was not to begin at the worst place, but at the most responsive and encouraging. By so doing he would be successful from the start, and the moral effect would be so great that the weaker places would then put forth their best effort to help themselves. It was his method to praise the worthy and teach, but not punish, the unworthy, and so he would like a comparatively good place to begin on, or otherwise he could not apply his methods to advantage. Hearing this, they chose Tsukahara and Oi, villages noted for the profligacy and sloth of the inhabitants. In this they were again influenced by their doubts. When Ninomiya heard their choice, he accepted it, but put off the undertaking indefinitely, for he felt that these men did not trust him, and he recognized that without their hearty cooperation his efforts would be handicapped. Ikeda felt this, too, and went back determined to remove their doubts, and inspire them with confidence in the man and his method.

It happened that, just at this time, a man named Takano was appointed assistant warden of the Soma districts. He was in hearty sympathy with the kind of work Ninomiya was doing, for he himself had tried to raise the villages of Narita and Tsubota, but for want of a proper method had failed. When Ikeda told him of Ninomiya's method, he requested permission to try it in the village under his care, and offered fifty hyo of his own rice to help defray the expenses. When the village chiefs heard this, they also offered to give either rice or money to help on the good work. They then took a census of the villages, estimated the number of acres of waste land, and sent Takano to Yedo to meet Ninomiya and invite him to put his method into operation. Ninomiya was very much pleased to begin work now, for he felt that in this movement there was evidence of true purpose. After explaining his method to Takano he sent one of his disciples home with him so that no time might be lost in getting to work. This was in the second year of Kokka (1845 A.D.). They began by picking out the best men, encouraging the less worthy, giving homes to the homeless, mending the roads, making the bridges and aqueducts, cultivating the wastes, and teaching the people humility and economy; in short, everywhere recommending simple, diligent, careful methods of living.

In a remarkably short time there was a great change in the people. Bad habits and customs were given up, and the villagers became prosperous. The retainers who formerly doubted were surprised at the change, and invited Ninomiya to apply the method all over the Soma estate, offering their hearty coöperation. They even apologized for their former rudeness, and openly acknowledged their mistake. In time the whole estate was restored to prosperity. From the second year of Kokka (1844 A.D.) to the fourth year of Meiji (1871 A.D.), a period of twenty years, 101 villages in Soma province adopted the method. Of these 55 became very prosperous, 46 were greatly improved, and the income of Soma was increased by 102,872 hyo, which was about 20,000 hyo more than it had ever been before. The number of houses was increased by 1135 and the people by 21,715, as shown by the official reports.

CHAPTER X

NINOMIYA AND YOUNG MEN

As Ninomiya's fame increased, he came to Yedo, and took up his abode in the house of Utsu, in Nishikubo. There he gathered disciples and taught them daily. Naturally he had opponents who were jealous of his power. They frequently pasted threats over his gate, to the effect that if any accepted his teaching their heads would be cut off, or they would be banished to a far-distant island, or their houses would be burned. His disciples became very scarce. Some excused themselves by saying they were busy, others who were boarding in his house fled home, but he only became the more earnest, and his spirit waxed stronger and stronger. He hung a picture of "Fudo Myo" [1] in his room, and pointing to it, said to his disciples, "Without such a spirit you are useless."

At one time, of all his disciples, only his brother Saburo Zayemon and his son Yataro remained. Once when he was giving them an important lec-

[1] This was a picture of the Buddhist God, with a drawn sword, standing or sitting unmoved in the midst of fire. Cf. note, page 100.

ture, they became sleepy and nodded; Ninomiya was very much annoyed, and said, "During these hard times of opposition, I am teaching you great truths, but you do not appreciate them as you should."

Ninomiya had a servant named Kosai Kamezo, from Echigo province. One day he asked him why he left such a fine province as Echigo and came to Yedo. He replied that it was not such a fine country, as the rice fields were dear, and the profits small. Yedo was a large city where money was easily obtained. Ninomiya answered: "You are mistaken; Echigo is a fine country, the soil is good, food plentiful, and the people numerous. The natural consequence is, that living is high and profits small. If Echigo were not a very fine country, it would be depopulated. You thought when you came to Yedo, because it is a large city, you were coming to a better place. That was foolish. If you now recognize your folly, you had better return to your native country, for there is not another country like it anywhere. There the ground worms are thick and large, but they are dissatisfied with the heat of the soil, and cry, 'Hot ! hot !' and come to the surface to get cool. But on the surface the heat of the sun is so excessive, they soon die. Their folly lay in leaving the soil. You are like the worm; you were not content to remain in Echigo, but must come up to the great city. I advise you to return to your natural element, the country." We are not told what the servant did.

Another servant, a relative of Ninomiya, was very poor, but desired to return home, and came to say good-by. Ninomiya advised him thus: "If you want to satisfy hunger, you must not give it first place. For example, if you go to a man and say, 'Give me something to eat and I'll sweep your garden for you,' you may be refused work; but if you say, 'Your garden needs cleaning; I'll sweep it for you,' and then go and sweep it well, even if you do not speak of reward he will likely give you something to eat. Such is human life; if you wish to succeed, you must unselfishly serve others. This must not take second place to anything. I learned this truth by experience. I was born in a very humble home, and possessed only one spade. One day when I broke it, I was perplexed to know what to do, so I asked the old man who lived next door to lend me his, but he was using it. I could not do anything till he was through, so I dug and sowed his garden for him. When this was done, the old man handed me the spade, telling me I was welcome to it as long as I needed it, and if I ever wanted anything he could lend me, he would be delighted to oblige me. My experience may be of value to you. You are a young man, and do not need to spend much time in bed. While others are still asleep, rise early and make straw sandals and other useful things. Then go where the laborer is at work and give them away. You need not care for the value, because you have made them in your leisure moments. Some men will accept them in silence without showing their appreciation, but so long as you are giving them something useful you need not care. Others will thank you over and over, while others will throw you a sen or two for your work. It does not matter what they give; that is not your responsibility. If you wish to succeed, you must give yourself without reserve to helping others."

One evening Ninomiya spoke to five or six young men as follows: "When people buy persimmons or pears at a low price, they examine them carefully. If they are not good, they refuse them, even if the price is only half a cent apiece. In the choice of young men, people are naturally even more careful. In the selection of a husband, an official, or a person for any position of honor, they choose carefully, and it depends on the quality of the man whether or not he is chosen. If he is the right kind of man, he will sooner or later be recognized. It does not matter how steep and dangerous the mountain slope may be, if there are mountain potatoes to be found on it, the people will find them. No matter how deep and muddy a hole may be, if it is known that eels are to be caught there, the people will get into the mud and search for them. So no matter where you were born or how lowly your station in life may be, if you are men of character, scholarship, and ability, you will be sought after. If you have no bad habits; do not become drunken with wine; do not visit places of questionable amusement; do not gamble and do not spend your time idly; but, on the contrary, if you are really noble in character, and making yourselves useful to men, you will be in demand. You must never think or speak hard of others because you are not being recognized, because if you are not, it is your own fault. Be what you can, do what you ought, and you need not worry about the result."

Ninomiya had a very interesting club of young men known as the "Imo-Arai-Kwai," potato washing bee. This meeting was not unlike a Methodist class meeting. The young men spoke freely of their mistakes, and gave expression to their desires and aspirations after better life. In the strongest Hotoku societies to-day they have this same kind of meeting, and many young men are helped by it. The name is derived from the custom that exists in Japan, of washing new potatoes by stirring them in a tub with a stick until they are clean.

Ninomiya hired a certain Chinese scholar to teach Chinese to the youngest students. This man gathered a very large class, and was having good success, but one day he became drunk with wine, and lay in the gutter, a filthy mass of vice, for under the influence of wine he was doing some shameful things. When his teaching hour came, to his surprise and anger there were no students. He protested to Ninomiya that although his conduct was not all that it should be, yet his teaching was important and necessary, for it was the teaching of the sages, and the young must learn it. Ninomiya said: "You are mistaken. Boiled rice is a very necessary and important food, but if you put it in a manure tub no one will eat it. So it is with your learning; you have put it in a manure tub, and even though it is the teaching of the sages, no one wants it from you. This is only natural." The teacher was very much humiliated, and resolved that henceforth both body and character should be kept pure, and fit to be the medium through which the noble teachings of the sages should pass down to young men.

Once when Ninomiya was in Sakuramachi, a rich and influential farmer, with his son, of whom he was very proud, came to consult him about sending the boy to the Seido, an educational institution of the Tokugawa age. Ninomiya said that, so far as it went, their plan was good, but that it depended largely on their motive whether their action was good or bad. He reminded the man of the good name of his family, of his own wealth and prosperity, and said that if their aim was to educate their boy so that after he had finished his course he would come back to be a more useful man, and help in lifting all the people into a higher plane of living, then education would be a great blessing to them, and their family would be a credit to their ancestors, whose name was already held in high esteem in that district. But if their motive was purely selfish, and if they wanted him to go to the Seido because they thought a farmer was very humble and insignificant, then they were mistaken in sending him at all. He told them that were they moved by selfish motives, their action would be followed by financial trouble and embarrassment, and would bring discredit on their family. The father and son did not like Ninomiya's words, and the boy went to school with their lower purposes in view. Some years after, the boy became a poor physician, and the old man was forced to part with his property, and spend his last days in a hand-to-mouth existence as a teacher of Japanese handwriting, in a country village.

One day a man named Gunji, who was pressed

for money, asked Saburo Zayemon to accompany him to Sakuramachi, to borrow one hundred yen from Ninomiya. When Ninomiya heard their request he told them, as it was the end of the year, he had little or no money on hand, but such as he had he would gladly lend them. He gave them eighty yen. They were afraid of being robbed on their way home, so Ninomiya made his brother a messenger of Lord Okubo, and gave him a messenger's disguise. Under the protection of this, they reached home safely, because the people respected the messenger of the feudal lord.[1]

When the two friends reached home, Gunji was still in a quandary as to how he was to raise the other twenty yen. Saburo was so sorry for him that he gave a lien on his own rice fields, and borrowed the money for him. When Saburo next met his brother, Ninomiya asked him how he managed to get the balance of the money. When Saburo told what he had done, Ninomiya was greatly moved and said, "My brother, you have become human for the first time."

[1] An old Japanese samurai told me that in his youth he once visited a friend in the employ of the Tokugawa family. Before he left the palace it became dark so he was given a lantern bearing the Tokugawa crest. On his way home, every one fell down before him because he carried the lantern bearing the crest of the military ruler of Japan.

CHAPTER XI

SOME OF HIS DISCIPLES

TOMIDA KOKEI, a samurai of the Soma clan, was an earnest student of Chinese classics in the Seido, a higher educational institution, situated in Hongo, Tokyo, on the present site of the Girls' Higher Normal School. Overstudy brought on brain trouble, so that he had to go to a doctor daily for treatment. One day when the doctor was not busy, they became engaged in conversation about Japan, and how to develop her resources and secure prosperity. Tomida was very earnest about the matter, and regretted that there was no competent teacher to instruct him, else he would gladly study methods of economy. A patient who overheard the conversation informed him that in Sakura-machi there was a famous teacher who was quite capable of giving him the instruction he desired. Thereupon Tomida sold his books and set out to seek Ninomiya. Ninomiya, however, refused to meet him, on the ground that Tomida being a scholar would have no need of instruction from a farmer, and no amount of persuasion could induce him to relent. One of Ninomiya's disciples took pity on him and invited him to his home. Here Tomida opened a school for young men, for he was determined not to leave the place until he had accomplished his purpose. For six months he remained, helping all who came to him, until his fame began to go abroad. Ninomiya, hearing of his work, sent him a kimono and a pair of trousers, and invited him to come into his presence. When Tomida arrived at Ninomiya's house, the first remark of the sage was, "They say you are a scholar; can you draw the Chinese character for bean?" Tomida took a paper brought to him by a servant and drew very skilfully the character for bean. Ninomiya examined it and asked, "Would a horse eat the bean you have drawn?" Tomida replied, "Perhaps not." Then Ninomiya, producing some real beans, said, "A horse will eat these." Tomida understood what Ninomiya intended to teach; viz., that mere theory would not save the nation, but that learning, to be of value, must be practical and useful. From this time he became the beloved disciple of Ninomiya, receiving his daughter Fumida in marriage.

Tomida was very proud of his learning, in spite of many rebukes from his master. One day he expressed great dissatisfaction with the treatment he received from heaven. He said his intentions were not selfish; his desire was to help his people

NINOMIYA RECEIVING.

and country. He was willing to work, and did work constantly, but he had a weak body, and heaven was responsible for that. Ninomiya replied that rats gnaw the shelves of the cupboard, cut holes in the ceiling, injure the furniture, and are always busy. When men sleep they work. From man's standpoint they are a nuisance, but from their own standpoint they are working for the best. It might be possible that Tomida was like the rat. He thought he was working for the best, but in the eyes of heaven his labors were poorly directed.

An interesting story is told about the first time Tomida started from home to attend the Seido in Tokyo. He had gone some distance on his way when he thought he heard a noise behind him. He looked around, and to his surprise there was his mother running after him, almost out of breath. He asked her what was the matter, and received the reply, "If you do not succeed, you need not return home." Such was the spirit of the mother of Ninomiya's greatest disciple. Such was and such is the spirit of many Japanese mothers. The mother of the famous Buddhist priest, Gen Shin Sozu, and the mother of the great scholar, Nakae Toju, were not unlike the mother of Tomida. This spirit is very likely due to the influence of the mother of Mencius.

Ninomiya said of the work that was being done

for the Soma estate, "It will succeed without fail, because there is a man named Tomita Kokei. We can tell what a bottle contains by merely tasting one drop of its contents, so by a little experience with this man I feel assured of the success of the Soma enterprise."

Saigo Takamori, one of the greatest leaders in the Revolution of 1868 A.D., trusted Tomita Kokei, and frequently sent his own disciples to him for instruction. Once Tomita asked Saigo how he came to know Ninomiya, who was comparatively little and unknown to the great. He replied that once when he went to visit Fujita Toko[1] at Mito, he had been told that if he wanted to study economic questions, he must consult Ninomiya. That was the first he had heard of him.

The Shibata family lived in Iwakamura, of Shizuoka prefecture. When they were prosperous, they had an income of eight hundred koku (about 4000 bushels) of rice, and eight storehouses in which to store it. Besides this, they had much mountain and bush land, and could enter the city of Shizuoka, which was seven miles from their home, without walking on any soil which they did not own. Such was the wealth of Junsaku's ancestors. In his home there was a rope that his family valued

---

[1] Fujita was strongly opposed to the opening up of Japan, and is well known for that reason.

very much. It was made from the wisteria vine and had been used in carrying heavy burdens on the back. On it were carved these words, "Our descendants must not forget the industrious spirit of their ancestors." But Junsaku's father failed in business, which together with the great famine of Tempo era left Junsaku in pretty hard circumstances. Fortunately he had a double pension for some services rendered by his ancestors to the government. He gave this to his father; but his own family were left in such destitution that his relatives gathered together to consult as to how best to relieve the financial strain. The family had 800 yen of credit outstanding, which was so old it would require government assistance to collect it, but Junsaku thought this would cause too much misery and suffering. A neighbor named Kuroganiya thus tried to force the payment of accounts. One old man on being pressed for payment drowned himself in the well. Kuroganiya gained nothing by his harsh methods, for he himself became very poor. Junsaku, knowing this, refused to follow the advice of his relatives. He was perplexed as to what to do, so he made a pretence of going to Izu hot springs, but instead went to Sunto township, to call on Mr. Kobayashi Heibei, who was a friend of the Shibata family and also a disciple of Ninomiya. He told Junsaku of Ninomiya's great work for deserted places, and offered to give him an introduction and obtain a loan for him, in which case they would set out early the following morning for Sakuramachi. Shibata thought it was a strange way to act, for his friends thought he had gone to the hot springs. He proposed to go home first and inform them of his intention. Kobayashi said that would not do; he must decide at once, and follow his advice; he must die to his past and henceforth live a new life. So Junsaku decided to go the following morning. On the way, at Isebara, near Odawara, they lodged at the house of Kato Sobei, of whom we have previously heard. Junsaku confidentially told Sobei they were going on a wild goose chase; Heibei was taking him to Ninomiya for advice. Sobei was displeased and said: "You are greatly mistaken. You are being guided by providence to one who is able to help you." Junsaku made no reply to this. When they arrived at Sakuramachi, Heibei left Junsaku in the coolies' shanty, while he himself went to Ninomiya to acquaint him with their errand. When Ninomiya heard the story, he said he had no message for such undecided people, and wondered at Heibei bringing such a person to him. This was an unexpected turn of events, so, not knowing what else to do, Junsaku was left in the shanty for the time being. While there he became interested in the great teacher and wished to hear him for himself. One day he was wandering about in the vicinity of Ninomiya's office, and hearing the teacher's voice, he listened, and found he could hear what was being said. After that he went often to listen, and the more he heard the more he wanted to hear, and the more he felt that Ninomiya's teaching was excellent and was all it had been represented by his friend. At the end of three weeks, Ninomiya suddenly asked to see Shibata, who immediately went and related his history in the presence of Heibei. Heibei also told what he knew of the Shibata family, repeating his request for a loan for Shibata from the "Hotoku" society. Ninomiya replied: "The cause of the decay of your family will be found in your own house, and if you want to restore the estate, you must learn to obey the methods of your ancestors. If you want to borrow money for the restoration, the case is hopeless, and it would be especially so if your spirit would allow you to oppress your old debtors. Let them be as they are." He then gave them two sayings; one of which was, "As we walk in an old path, pushing to either side the accumulated leaves of trees, we may see the traces of the god of Heaven." The other was, "Thinking of the former whiteness, wash a cloth repeatedly, and it will become white

again." Giving them ten yen, Ninomiya bade
Junsaku return home. He went, intending to put
Ninomiya's teaching into practice, but found that
he lacked the ability to do so. He decided he must
go and hear the teaching again, so he consulted his
wife and mother about it. Receiving their consent,
he set out for Sakuramachi, where, by the help of
Heibei, he became a cook. Heibei, fearing Junsaku
had returned too soon, did not tell Ninomiya of
his arrival, and it was some time before his presence
was discovered. When he did hear of it, Ninomiya
was not displeased, but shortly afterwards made
Junsaku waiter at his own table. For four years
he remained at this work, during which time he was
once severely reprimanded. He served Ninomiya
pickled radish which was not cut clean through, so
that when Ninomiya tried to pick up a piece with
his chopsticks, all the radish on the plate came with
it. Ninomiya held the radish up, and asked
Junsaku whether he had intended to cut it
through. He said such things indicate indecision
and carelessness. A man with such a disposition
cannot be a success. Ninomiya refused to eat the
radish, and Shibata felt much humiliated and made
what apology he could. Ninomiya wished to
impress upon him the importance of thoroughness
and care. Another time Ninomiya praised him for
a deliciously seasoned dish of beans.

While Junsaku was away, his wife worked very hard to support the other members of the family. The relatives held another consultation and ordered Junsaku to return home. At first he refused, but finally consented to go back. He had no funds, so he used to get up early, and carry tow for making fire with flint and steel, and on his return bring back a load of paper. Thus he earned coolie's wages, and for the time was content, because he remembered the teaching he had received from Ninomiya. He did this for five years, and out of his scanty earnings he managed to save a little. Then the price of land rose, and some of his debtors were able to pay their loans. In this way he began to be more prosperous. He wrote to one of Ninomiya's servants telling of his increasing prosperity, and expressing his gratitude. This letter fell into the hands of Ninomiya, who was greatly delighted, and showed it to his disciples and told them how one who had followed his methods had been rewarded by success. He said, "If we sow, we shall surely reap."

One day the children were out playing their New Year's games. All except Shibata's little daughter were gayly dressed. She ran to her mother begging for a better kimono, but her mother told her that as her father was endeavoring to follow the teachings of Ninomiya, and thus restore their property, they could not possibly afford to give her anything better. The little girl did not understand her parents' struggle, and coaxed for a new dress, but her father and mother would not give way to her coaxing.

Some time after this Shibata heard that Ninomiya was at Hakone, and determined to visit him, as it was five years since he had seen him. He arrived at Hakone at 11 o'clock at night, and as Ninomiya had retired, he had to wait until morning to see him. Ninomiya was glad to renew his acquaintance, and said: "I am very glad indeed to see you. I heard of your successful struggles from my servant to whom you wrote." Although Ninomiya had planned an early start, out of respect for Shibata he spent the day in Hakone talking with him and giving him helpful suggestions. Shortly after this Shibata organized a "Hotoku" society in his own village, for which he worked very earnestly. In the ninth year of Meiji (1876 A.D.) he was made President of the "East Suruga Hotoku Society."

One morning when Shibata was carrying his load of tow, he had to pass through a very lonely place called Shiroyama. Here he suddenly met a "Tengu."[1] He thought to himself, "This is 'Tengu

[1] Tengu is an imaginary being supposed to frequent mountains and forests. It is represented in pictures with a red face, a long nose, and a pair of wings. One man told me that he once saw one. It was like moving fire and frightened him so badly that he

Sama,'" but he was so conscious of being in the path of duty, he felt very little fear, and thus boldly addressed the fiery elf: "I am working in all sincerity. My heart is true, and my purpose is unselfish, for I seek neither honor nor pleasure. Try my heart and see." No sooner had he said this than the fire quickly disappeared.

Fukuzumi, a famous disciple of Ninomiya, was the wealthy owner of a well-known bath-house at Hakone. One time when he was in the bathroom with Ninomiya, the latter said: "Rich men are never satisfied. The more money they have, the more they want. They are like me in regard to the water in this tub; when it reaches only to my waist, I wish it would reach my head. But if I fill it so full, others,[1] especially children, cannot get into it without danger." Another time Ninomiya pushed the water away from him with the palms of his hands, but when it reached the edge of the tub it came back around him higher than

hid his face with fear. He added, "I know that there is a scientific explanation for it, but truly there are strange things." He told me about an old man in the Nikko Mountains who was surprised to see his bath move out of the bathroom. He cried out, "O Tengu San, please forgive me." Thereupon the Tengu moved his bath back into the room. They were supposed at times to carry men off and hide them.

[1] A Japanese bath-house is supplied with several basins so that each person may sponge his body clean before getting into the large tub which is used by everybody. In this way several people use the same water.

ever. Drawing his companions' attention to this, he said, "This is the way with men. If they give themselves and all they have to men, they will reap the highest benefit. But if, casting away love, they become selfish, and try to draw the water all around themselves, it will resist their efforts, and they will fail. So we must give our best to others, if we would expect the best for ourselves."

"If a man says, 'I am going to become a sage,' he will certainly fail. If he works for humanity, according to his heavenly truth, earnestly serving his parents and his country, possessing charity for others, then, whether he wills it or not, others will call him a sage, though he himself is scarcely aware of the fact. It will resemble the saying, 'They say he is a sage. He is a sage. I thought, who is a sage? It was Confucius who lived next door to me.'" Ninomiya said he had once had such an experience. He went to the city of Hatogoya to visit Sanshi, of whom he had heard great reports, but when he arrived there he could not find the famous teacher. Finally, after asking many people, one man said: "It must be Shobei, a teacher of Japanese, who helps the children. He lives over yonder on the back street." This was the very man he was searching for. Shobei was Sanshi's popular name.

Kenmochi Hirokichi was a man of Sobi village, in

Sagami province, about a mile from Kayama, the birthplace of Ninomiya. He was twenty-two years of age when he first met Ninomiya. Both were accustomed to go to Odawara on business, and on one of these trips they chanced to meet, and became interested in each other. Although Kenmochi was only a peasant, he had some learning, having been taught by a Buddhist priest and by a Chinese scholar. He wrote both Japanese and Chinese poems, and could even read the Buddhist scriptures. After his interview with Ninomiya, he said: "I am a scholar by study; Ninomiya is a scholar by nature. I am one taught by a teacher; Ninomiya is taught by nature. Consequently I was no match for him in discussion." Kenmochi, though favorably impressed, did not become a disciple of Ninomiya until long after this first meeting. His brother-in-law, Konai, often urged him to study Hotoku, but he always refused, saying, "You are talking nonsense, what does he know?" Hirokichi was advised to try the methods of Hotoku in Sobi, which had become very poor. He finally agreed to go and consult Ninomiya, who at the time was staying at a hotel in Hakone. When he reached the hotel, Ninomiya was taking a bath, so, being an old friend, he went to the bathroom, but to his surprise Ninomiya turned his back on him. He immediately left the bathroom and began to drink wine, saying to himself: "Ninomiya's head is turned with the honor that is being shown to him; he is proud and impolite and does not recognize his old friends." A long time after this, he was again persuaded to go to Ninomiya, and again received similar treatment, but being urged to persevere, he proceeded to Ninomiya's hotel, arriving there just as Ninomiya was removing his sandals. To his surprise, Ninomiya gave him a cordial welcome, and invited him to take a bath. After the bath they talked till midnight. They went together to the home of Uzawa at Odawara. Here Ninomiya said to him: "How about the village of Sobi? Is it still poor? The poor of that village are your responsibility." · Hirokichi said the burden was too heavy for him to carry alone. Ninomiya threw him his sword, saying, "Take this and go to the richest man in Odawara and rob him; there may be no other means of helping them." Hirokichi proposed that they organize societies called "Mujinko," in which each man puts in a regular amount each month, and then all draw lots to see who may receive the whole sum of money thus collected. Ninomiya asked if the fortunate man would drop out of the club after receiving the money. Such a society, he thought, would be an evil. For several days and nights, Hirokichi worried over the problem of rescuing this village.

He became so exhausted that Ninomiya ordered the official to give him some money that he might take a rest. Hirokichi stayed at Odawara, and rested on official funds. When he returned to Ninomiya, the latter again impressed upon him his responsibility for Sobi village. Seven years later the village had been rescued by the method of "Hotoku," through the work of Hirokichi, and it became a very prosperous place. In a poem written by an official at the time, the change is described as one from the desolation of winter to the beauty of spring. Lord Odawara praised him, giving him a present in recognition of the good work done. Hirokichi became the village chief. He had saved not only his own estate, but those of the whole village.

CHAPTER XII

THE LAST GREAT WORK OF NINOMIYA

WHEN Tokugawa Iyeyasu died, his bones were interred at Kuno about seven miles from the city of Shizuoka. Afterwards they were divided, and a part of them placed in Nikko, which thereupon became an important place to the Tokugawa family and as a result the Tokugawa government made Nikko[1] very beautiful.

In addition to beautifying the immediate vicinity of the temples, the Tokugawa family was anxious that the villages in the district should become prosperous, and that the people should be industrious and moral. The soil around these villages was difficult to cultivate, and since the great famine of Tenmei the condition of the people had gradually become worse, and the villages depopulated. In the first year of Kokka (1844 A.D.) the government asked Ninomiya to take charge and improve these villages. At the end of about three years'

---

[1] At Nikko may be seen the most beautiful scenery in Japan. The Japanese say if you have not seen Nikko, do not say "splendid" of any scenery.

investigation he presented to the government his plans for the improvement of the district, in sixty Japanese volumes. After this he became the servant of the Mokka municipality, and put his method into successful operation for the reformation of several of their villages.

In the sixth year of Kaei, in February, the Tokugawa government ordered the plans submitted by Ninomiya put into execution; unfortunately, in April of that year (1853 A.D.) Ninomiya took sick, and was ill for several months. He was so anxious to help the people of these villages that in spite of his weak condition and against the advice of his friends, he went to Nikko to begin the work. At this time he was in his sixty-seventh year, but during the heat of summer he visited the whole district, and studied its need. To the poorest of the people he gave one to five ryo each; to two of the villages he gave eighty and fifteen ryo, respectively. Everywhere he went he preached and taught the duty of man, emphasizing filial piety, honesty, righteousness, and brotherly love. The money he received for the work he deposited along with some of his own, and used only the interest. In February of the seventh year of Kaei (1854 A.D.) the government ordered Ninomiya's oldest son to assist him in managing the work, and from that time till his death, father and son worked together. They built waterways to irrigate[1] the fields, bringing the water from the Daiya River along both banks, for miles. During the time this work was going on, he continued his usual methods, praising the worthy, teaching the wicked, giving homes to the homeless, lending money without interest to those who were in debt, supplying farm implements until the people could afford to buy new, and teaching them the dignity and importance of toil, and of mutual help. In this way he and his son went about doing good, and their noble spirit, example, and work brought about better conditions among the people. The deserted part of Nikko contained about 2000 cho (circa 5000 acres), of which about one-fourth had been irrigated and brought under cultivation, when he took sick, and died on the 20th of October in the third year of Ansei (1856 A.D.), at the age of seventy-one years.

After his death, his teaching and methods were studied by an ever increasing body of men, until to-day his followers are scattered all over Japan. It is not an unusual thing to see large gatherings of peasants assembled to study his teachings.

A story is told that when Ninomiya was ordered

[1] The system of irrigation in Japan is highly developed; rivers are tapped and the water is sometimes brought through tunnels under mountains. The aqueducts are provided with sluice gates to regulate the supply of water for the fields.

to do this work at Nikko, he sighed, and said, "My intention is to refine human kind rather than to restore deserted wastes, but now I am again ordered to do the latter." He thought that it was very important to restore deserted places, but that it was much more important to teach and develop men. He used to say, "If we would only develop the deserted wastes in human minds, we could then let the deserted fields look out for themselves."

[1] On his death-bed he gave orders that his funeral was not to be an expensive one, and that his disciples were not to raise a costly monument over his grave, but, having raised a mound of earth, they were to plant a pine or a cedar tree to mark the place. After his death his disciples were divided into two groups, one wishing to build a fine monument, and the other wishing to adhere strictly to Ninomiya's request. Finally, however, a monument and a shrine were built at Imaichi, near Nikko, and another at Odawara.

Time tends to weave a garland of tradition and myth around the lives of great men, especially those who have entered most fully into the religious and moral life of man, and although Ninomiya lived in the last century, there is some evidence

---

[1] The efforts that are being made to-day by followers of Ninomiya to honor him with expensive shrines and festivals are completely contrary to the spirit of the great man. They honor him most who practise his teachings.

already that he will be no exception to the general rule. Among the many stories that are told about him, there are some that are shrouded in mystery.

One evening shortly after he first went to Saku-ramachi, while he was taking a bath, a young man suddenly and mysteriously appeared, and in an excited voice and manner said: "Teacher, you are in danger. Get out of the bath." So saying, he left the room as quickly as he had entered it, and was not seen again. Ninomiya, fearing treachery, hurried to dress himself, but before he had finished, two spears were thrust through the thin wall above the bathtub from which he had just escaped.

There is another story that when he was only fourteen years of age, he was on his way to the temple of the Goddess of Mercy, at the village of Iizumi, when a pilgrim suddenly appeared to him and began to teach him the sacred scriptures of this goddess. When he had been fully taught, the pilgrim disappeared as mysteriously as he had come.

Once when Ninomiya's brother, Saburo Zayemon, came on a visit, he was very cordially welcomed, but immediately after, Ninomiya became very uneasy and advised him to hasten home, as he had a strange impression that his house was in danger of being burned. Saburo yielded to his brother's entreaty and set out for home at once. On arriving there he found that, sure enough, fire had broken out,

GODDESS OF MERCY.

and already the straw mats were almost destroyed. Giving the alarm, he succeeded in saving his belongings, but had he been an hour later all would have been lost.

In the home of Mr. Ozawa, north of Odawara castle, there is said to be a very fine old statue of Ninomiya, holding a copy of the great learning in one hand, and a fan in the other. During the life of Ninomiya he saw this, and advised them to put a large knife in his hand instead of the fan, to indicate that if Confucius taught anything contrary to human good, he would cut it out. His friends thought the knife might give a wrong impression, so they continued to use the fan.

The attitude taken by Ninomiya toward the foreign ships that were frequently coming to Japan was very naïve. One of his ardent admirers quoted him as saying: "Trade with foreign countries was forbidden by Iyeyasu. We must strictly obey the government's order. But seeing they have come from far America to trade with Japan, there must be some lack in America. We have a very good country. It has a good climate. There is nothing lacking in Japan, so that it is very natural for them to come to us from America. If, however, we fire on them without reserve, it is very cruel. On the other hand, we cannot supply the whole world. It is impossible, because we have so many deserted places. When these waste places are cultivated and a great surplus is accumulated, we may be able to share with them, and that will probably satisfy them. But at present we have not plenty. We must tell them to wait awhile. If they do not obey us, then there is nothing else to do but fire on them. When I went to restore Sakura-machi, some of the people of Aoki village opposed me. I gave them some houses and stables, and they were thankful and obeyed me. Humanity throughout the world is the same. A singing girl once said in a song, 'Even in Ezo and Matsumae [uncivilized places of Ninomiya's time] the human mind is not different to ours.' This saying explains the nature of the human mind; therefore if we show the people of the United States kindness, even they will not come with the sword. The policy of unreserved opposition is not good."

PART II

THE TEACHINGS OF NINOMIYA SONTOKU

CHAPTER I

"HOTOKU"—MAKING RETURNS FOR BLESSINGS RECEIVED

THE teachings of Ninomiya are mostly found in his "Evening Addresses," in which, however, no attempt is made to systematize them. In the following chapters the most important paragraphs are arranged systematically, placing before us the leading ideas of this man and his society.

The fundamental teaching of Ninomiya is known as "Hotoku" (literally, "The Rewarding of Graces"). The sage bases his teachings both on ethics and economy upon the central doctrine of making return to heaven, earth, and man for the benefits received from them.

The following quotations, which are in effect translations of his original words, give us an idea of what he felt and taught.

In his "Evening Addresses" he says: "My teaching is that we should reward grace and virtue. If asked for an explanation, I would say this means that we make return to heaven, man, and earth for the gracious benefits we have received from them. Heaven's blessing is given in the light of the sun and moon. The sun rises and sets. The four seasons come and go. In every living creature there is both development and decay. In these and other ways heaven's blessing is manifested toward us. Earth manifests her favor in the growth of grasses, trees, and grain; in the fact that birds, animals, and fish live. Man's grace is manifested in the fact that sages teach the truth; emperors govern their subjects; high officials protect the country and people; farmers raise our food; mechanics build our homes; and merchants distribute commodities. We all live by the grace of heaven, earth, and man, and so we must make it our first principle of conduct to make return to them for their gracious contributions to our welfare. From H. I. Majesty the Emperor down to the humblest peasant this spirit must prevail. Every one who is, according to his heavenly gift, living within his means, by industry and economy, by saving his surplus money as a fund for restoring and developing deserted wastes, paying debts, rescuing the poor, helping villages and provinces, by saving home after home, village after village, until, all Japan having become prosperous, the prosperity shall spread to foreign countries, is making return for the blessings he has received from heaven, earth, and man."

There was an abridged creed of the Hotoku[1] Society called "Sansai-Hotoku-Kun." This was used to keep before the members of the society the main teachings of Ninomiya. Being translated, it means: "The origin of our parents[2] is the command of heaven and earth. The origin of the body lies in the nurture of the parents. The succession of descendants depends upon the painstaking efforts of husband and wife. The wealth of our parents depends upon the industry of their ancestry, and our wealth depends upon the accumulated good deeds of our parents. Our descendants' wealth depends upon us and our faithful discharge of duty. Long life depends upon food, raiment, and habitation. Raiment, food, and habitation depend upon rice fields, uplands, mountains, and woods. These again depend upon the people's industry. This year's clothing and food depend upon last year's labor. Next year's food and clothing depend upon this year's struggle. Year after year, generation after generation, 'Hotoku' must not be forgotten."

Ninomiya said: "In 'Kokyo' (the Chinese classic on filial piety) it is said that God rejoices in a man of extreme filial piety, and that his influence is felt

[1] Literally, teaching about making return to heaven, earth, and man for their favor.
[2] Cf. below Rules, Article III.

by all. Now I will simplify this for you. Filial
piety is the duty of making return to our parents for
their goodness to us. A younger brother should
make return to his older brother for his favor. If
we know that we ought to make return for the
blessings we receive, we have learned a very important principle. Speaking of making return
for the blessings we receive, we may say it is the
interest on borrowed money, thanks for favors received, value for articles bought, wages for the
laborer's toil. We must look upon the benefits
we have received in this way, and make return to
heaven, earth, and man for them. If we do this,
we shall be able to accomplish anything we wish.
This is a joy to God and gives our fellow-men pleasure in our conduct, and confidence in our words."

"Take good heed to this principle, of making
return for grace. There are many cases where it
is neglected, and grace has gone unnoticed. If you
forget the blessings [1] received from the past, and
think only of future blessing, you will certainly
lose your joy. But if you are mindful of past blessings, even if you do not think of the future, you
will naturally become happy and prosperous.
Therefore making return for past blessings is the
foundation of all good deeds. Remember that the
origin of our bodies lies in the nurture of our

[1] Literally, "grace."

parents, who originated in the love of our grand-
parents, and if we go back far enough we will come
to the gracious command of heaven and earth.
Heaven and earth are our great parents. Again
every one wishes for long life, because he believes
that to-morrow and the next day the sun will rise.
If man did not believe in the permanence of present conditions, he would not wish to live. Therefore we see that heaven and earth are even now
bountifully bestowing their grace upon us in giving
permanence to all things."

"My teaching emphasizes making return for
blessings received by good deeds. We have received great and abundant blessings from heaven,
earth, the Emperor, our parents, and our ancestors.
We must show our appreciation of these in our
good works. Toward the Emperor we call it
loyalty, toward our parents we call it filial piety,
etc. When any one wishes to become my disciple,
I teach him the importance of keeping well within
his means and of limiting his expenses; I also
teach him that his salary is a heavenly gift intrusted
to him. Such teaching is very necessary, because
most of the sons of the rich do not know the value
of their property nor how to live within their means.
So I ask them how many rice fields they have, how
many mountains, how much bush land, how much
debt, how much they realize from their property,

how much income they need, how much they lay aside for good works, and how much they use for their families. In this way I examine their income and teach them that it is a heavenly gift. I teach them that with that income they must pay the demands of society, and if it is insufficient they must withdraw from society. Unless we fix a limit to our expenditures, we cannot do good deeds, for if a man is always poor and in debt he cannot do his best."

"Man is born and lives his life peacefully by the three graces mentioned above. In the world there is the law of recompense, which demands that we make return for these blessings; for example, obedience is the recompense we render for the grace of our parents, and disobedience is punished by the government. Taxes and faithful service are the recompense we render for the grace of the Emperor. But heaven and earth demand no recompense, therefore all people high and low neglect to offer them their true recompense. We find teachings here and there, but they only produce ceremony and form, and these are insufficient. True recompense is to obey the heavenly will, to develop heavenly gifts, and to coöperate with heaven in bringing about a better world."

"When people have no food for the morrow, they go to their neighbors for help, and if they come to such a pass that they cannot get food by any means, they usually leave the kettle, tray, and bowls all unwashed. This illustration probably describes the spirit of most men, but it is the spirit that leads to poverty. We should not wash the dishes merely because we expect to use them to-morrow, but we should wash them out of gratitude for having been able to use them to-day. Even if we are to die of starvation we must wash the dishes, giving thanks for the blessings we have received up to the present. If we have this spirit of gratitude, there is no doubt of our having food and plenty, for that spirit is in harmony with the will of heaven. Riches and poverty are not absolute distinctions. The man who thinks only of to-morrow will be poor, but if he has true gratitude for the blessings of the past he will gradually become rich. We must carefully bear this important truth in mind. Buddhists say this world is temporary, and an illusion, and that the future is important. Yes, the future is very important, but it is a mistake to say that this life is temporary and unimportant. Take for illustration a piece of grass. Its seed is very important for the future, but if we want good seed we must nourish the grass now. If we neglect the grain when it is growing, we cannot get good seed. So if we wish to enjoy the future life, we must do good deeds now. If we wish for paradise, we must do good now and cast out evil intention and desire. The present is not an illusion because the happiness of the future depends upon it. We have Emperor, parents, wives, and children in this life. Buddha threw away the present life and tried to rescue others from it. That was his great mistake."

"Everything is determined by heaven. We cannot go too near a great fire, but if the fuel be exhausted the fire will naturally die out. Flying arrows or bullets are dangerous, but if they have spent their force, they may be picked up with perfect safety. So no man possesses great power in himself alone. He owes it to his ancestors, or to the authority of officials. Without the backing of others, man has no power, but is like the arrow or the bullet when they have spent their force."

CHAPTER II

IT was while Ninomiya was engaged in the great work at Sakuramachi that he first gave his disciples the teachings of Hotoku; he himself became known as the Hotoku teacher, and his method as the Hotoku method. An office was established at Soma, and another at Odawara. The latter was closed at the death of the lord of Odawara; the former continued until the beginning of the Meiji (circa 1868). Later, one of his leading disciples wished to unite Hotoku and Shintoism, thereby forming a branch of Shinto to be known as the Hotoku Association. In the fifth year of Meiji (1872 A.D.) this was forbidden by the Home Department, because, in a semi-religious association, the true meaning of Hotoku would not be properly represented. The society of Hotoku, as we see it to-day, was first organized in the Tempo Era (some time between 1830 and 1843 A.D.) in Hitachi province, in the city of Shimodate. It gradually spread until it entered Totomi and Suruga, two counties in Shizuoka prefecture, which

at present are its strongholds. There are also societies in Hiroshima, Niigata, and Nagano prefec-
tures. Immediately after the Russo-Japanese War
there were in Japan about 600 societies, with a
membership of about 26,000, and a capital of about
600,000 yen. In Kagoshima and Miyazaki pre-
fectures the society is not popular, so the societies
there are few, and the funds small, but great efforts are made to purify the moral life and customs
of the people by means of its teaching. The real
influence of Hotoku is not adequately represented
by the above small figures. As stated in the pref-
ace, the popularity of the society has been greatly
augmented since the Russo-Japanese War and is
becoming more and more influential among the
farming and merchant classes.

Ninomiya thought that great benefit might be
derived from the united efforts of good men. He
believed that while it was a good thing to reform
the individual, it was a better thing to unite men
in the interest of the country, and society in general. Hence came the organization of Hotoku
with its twofold object: first, to develop morality;
second, to promote industry and economy. The
plan of the society was to lay aside a fund from
which loans could be made to members and others
who were struggling with debt or other unfavorable
circumstances. This fund could also be used to

improve poor or neglected homes or villages, to start new industries and enterprises, and for public works, such as building or repairing bridges, roads, etc. The following general rules will help to a better understanding of the society as it exists to-day in Japan.

GENERAL RULES

ARTICLE I.

Any one wishing to enter the society must fulfil the following conditions : —

(1) He must show by his good deeds gratitude to the gods, the Emperor, his parents, and his ancestors for their grace.

(2) He must be industrious and economical, living according to his means, and holding up a standard of conduct that will tend toward his own and his country's prosperity.

(3) He must sow good seed, plant good roots, and thus he will enjoy eternal happiness.

ARTICLE II.

(1) Hotoku is not a religion, but a system of morality based on philosophy, discountenancing mere speculation.

(2) The two words "Ho-toku" (literally, "reward for grace") signify : —

(a) The endeavor to assimilate all that is good in Japan and foreign countries.

(*b*) The effort to unite the higher and the lower classes, the wise and the simple.

(*c*) The aim to combine the teaching of this world and that of the future world.

ARTICLE III.

When a meeting of the society is in session, the tablet of Amaterasu[1] O-Mikami shall be hung on the wall at the front of the room ; on the left side the statue of Ninomiya, called "Hotoku-kun"; or the chart for teaching industry; or the chart of "Bunnai"; which emphasizes living according to one's means. In front of the picture of Amaterasu shall be placed sacred wine and food. This ceremony shall be properly reverenced. The members as they enter shall bow before it.

ARTICLE IV.

The Hotoku Society shall endeavor to put into practice the best elements of Shintoism, Confucianism, and Buddhism, and although only the picture of Amaterasu hangs on our walls, the others are not thereby rejected. The national spirit shall be considered of first importance, and may be represented as the head, the other teachings as the wings.

---

[1] The Sun Goddess, the root from which the present Imperial Family are supposed to have sprung.

THE GOD TABLET.

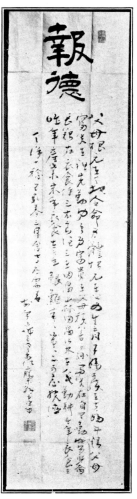

THE ABRIDGED CREED OF
THE HOTOKU SOCIETY.

Useless investigation shall be rejected and practical works exalted.

ARTICLE V.

Hotoku shall hold no relation to religion, yet it shall oppose any religion that is injurious to the nation. It shall make every effort to dispel superstition and spread the light of truth.

ARTICLE VI.

In accordance with Ninomiya's method (called Bundo) of keeping the expenditure well within the income, this society shall require each member to lay aside one quarter of his income as a surplus. If any member finds this impossible, allowance shall be made to meet his case.

ARTICLE VII.

While it is important that the households of the members be as far as possible organized with a view to economy, yet the purpose of this society shall not interfere with the private affairs of the home. Moreover, while the members shall be interested in reforming the policy of their respective villages, unless they be elected to official positions, they shall not interfere with those who are officials.

ARTICLE VIII.

This society shall hold no relation to any political party; nor shall it assume any responsibility for the actions of any of its members who belong to one or other of the political parties. It shall emphasize only loyalty to the Empire.

ARTICLE IX.

Each society shall hold a monthly public meeting, at which practical subjects shall be discussed, and lectures given on industrial, educational, hygienic, or ethical subjects.

ARTICLE X.

At all such open meetings the Hotoku-Kun shall be read, followed by a reverent bow. Every member shall be able to recite the Hotoku-Kun from memory.

ARTICLE XI.

The funds of the society shall be divided into "Foundation Money" and "Good Seed Money." The members shall help to increase these funds by seeking to spread the influence of the society and by practising industry and economy, so that by increasing their own wealth they may be able to donate money to the society.

ARTICLE XII.

Teachers and officers of the society who prove themselves men of merit shall have their names reported at the shrine of Ninomiya, and shall be presented with a copy of "Hotoku-Dendo." This privilege shall also be open to members who get an intelligent grasp of Hotoku and practise it diligently.

ARTICLE XIII.

The funds of the society shall be disposed of as follows : —

(*a*) The Foundation Money, which shall consist of voluntary offerings of the members, and of registration fees, shall be used for running expenses, rewarding good deeds with prizes, for public works, for new industries, for the relief of distress caused by disaster such as earthquakes, typhoons, etc.; and to build offices and rooms for the society, or to help start branch societies.

(*b*) The Good Seed Money, which shall consist of the surplus funds of the members, shall be loaned to members on the vote and recommendation of the society, to be used for any worthy enterprise. The fund shall be open to farmers, merchants, and mechanics alike.

(*c*) The thank-offering money consists of money given in gratitude for money borrowed from the society, and is added to the Good Seed Fund and allowed to accumulate.

(*d*) The surplus is of two kinds; viz., extra pay for extra work; and money saved on clothing, food, furniture, etc. Each member is expected to donate at least ten sen per month. Fifty yen is one share. Rich men may buy as many shares as they wish, but every member is expected to continue his monthly payments until he has at least one share. Any member withdrawing from the society cannot take back his money. The Good Seed Money is allowed to accumulate *ad infinitum*.

ARTICLE XIV.

Every Hotoku society shall have a Foundation Fund, and a Good Seed Fund, whatever other special funds they may have.

ARTICLE XV.

These several funds shall not be interchanged.

ARTICLE XVI.

Regulations of sub-societies.

ARTICLE XVII.

(*a*) Loans shall be returned without delay after the date of expiration. Money shall not be subloaned. Money shall not be loaned without full investigation of the conditions of the place, the profession and standing of the man who borrows.

(*b*) Ninomiya taught that Heaven lends us many things without interest, therefore he was opposed to the payment of interest. But suppose a member borrows fifty yen, he might repay it in ten yearly payments of five yen each, but the eleventh year he was supposed to bring another five yen as a thank-offering, saying, —

"By the aid of Hotoku I have received great benefit, so I bring this thank-offering." The thank-offering always corresponded to the yearly refund.

ARTICLE XVIII.

Societies organized in villages and towns shall receive official sanction from the parent society, and the members shall receive certificates from the same. Should such societies wish to receive government recognition, they shall do so through the parent society.

ARTICLE XIX.

Each society shall have some distinguishing name.

ARTICLE XX.

Rural societies shall receive official sanction for a period of sixty years' duration. This period may be prolonged or shortened to suit peculiar conditions. No society shall be organized without time limitation except in very extreme cases. Sanction shall not be given for a period of less than ten years.

ARTICLE XXI.

All Hotoku organizations shall enter the union of Hotoku societies. The constitution of each branch shall bear the seal of the President of the Union.

ARTICLE XXII.

Upon the organization of a new society the charter members shall diligently promote the interests of the society for at least five years.

ARTICLE XXIII.

Evil customs observed to exist in the neighborhood of a Hotoku society shall be written at the end of the constitution, and, by keeping them ever in mind, the members shall endeavor to correct them.

ARTICLE XXIV.

The funds [1] shall be carefully administered, and the bookkeeping must be safe.

ARTICLE XXV.

The books of the village and city societies shall be as carefully kept as those of the parent society.

ARTICLE XXVI.

Two or more persons shall constitute a society. Applicants for membership shall fulfil the conditions laid down in Article I before receiving a certificate of membership.

[1] The Hotoku Society holds its funds through a "Shadan Hojin," an organization for holding property.

Article XXVII.

All information in reference to this society may be had in the Great Japan Hotoku Report, of which all societies shall have a copy.

Article XXVIII.

At present the teaching of Hotoku is making progress, not because it is specially favored, but because of the standard of its teaching ; not because of its finances, but because of its standard of conduct. Therefore it shall not be considered as a bank, but as an ethical society.

Article XXIX.

Trusts have to do with money. Hotoku has first to do with morals. But as economy is an important factor in society, the societies shall, by adopting the hard and fast rules of a trust company, endeavor to assist in all questions of social economy.

Article XXX.

Any person entering the society shall be presented by the parent society with a metal badge of membership. Special merit shall be rewarded with a gold or silver badge.

Article XXXI.

The parent society shall present each member

with a book called "Katei Kai Kihan," [1] which they shall be expected to follow.

ARTICLE XXXII.

Should any trouble arise between any members of a sub-society, which is likely to bring harm to the society, the case shall be handled by the president of that society in consultation with the parent society. Should trouble arise in the parent society, the officials of that society shall be empowered to deal with it.

ARTICLE XXXIII.

Should any member be suspended for objectionable conduct, he must first obtain the permission of the parent society before he can again become a member in good standing.

ARTICLE XXXIV.

Similar societies organized in other districts, or members from other districts wishing to enter the Hotoku Society shall follow the rules herein prescribed. Any such society, becoming very prosperous, shall be made a branch of this society.

ARTICLE XXXV.

Should a society of another district not wish to adopt our constitution, our relation to them shall still be friendly. Should they need it we will stand

[1] Family rules.

in an advisory relation to them, and if they will not hear us, our affiliation (literally, " our friendly relationship ") shall cease.

ARTICLE XXXVI.

Any member of such a friendly society who gains an understanding knowledge of the teachings of Hotoku shall, if he so desires, be presented with a copy of "Hotoku Dendo," and he may become a member of the parent society.

ARTICLE XXXVII.

Any person wishing to organize a society, not strictly Hotoku, but along similar lines, shall omit Part 2 of Article II, and he may amend other rules as he may see fit.

CHAPTER III

In his relation to the older religions, Ninomiya has been called an eclectic. In a sense he is, but unlike most advocates of the older religions he has an independent and original standpoint from which he is able to reject what does not appeal to him. The universe was his unwritten sacred book, and he rejected anything that he considered out of harmony with it. The fact that he was able to do this makes his estimate of other religions very valuable. The following quotations, although they may involve some repetition, will give the substance of his thought more accurately than any statement which could be made of his teaching.

"There is only one 'Way' in the world. Shintoism, Buddhism, and Confucianism are only so many gates by which we may enter this way. The Tendai, Shingon, Hokke, Zen, and other sects of Buddhism are but so many smaller paths leading to the same great way. The relation of these various sects to truth may be illustrated in this way: There is a stream of pure, clear water; several men throw in coloring matter, one green, another indigo, another purple or red, each man thinking his own color the best. But if this discolored water be thrown out on the ground and allowed to soak through the soil into the stream again, it will be as pure as the stream at its fountainhead. So these various sects are not essentially different. It is a mistake to think there are different truths in this world. There are many ways to climb Mount Fuji. You may take a path from Yoshida, or from Subashiri, or from Suyama. If you follow any of these paths, you will eventually reach the summit, but there is only one summit. So there are many ways, but if they do not lead to the one truth, they are false. We must be careful not to be deceived by false teachers who lead earnest souls astray."

"Thinking over the weak points of Buddhism, Confucianism, and Shintoism, I wrote, 'In this social world there are weak people and strong people, just as there are long piles and short piles driven in to protect the river bank.' Shintoism teaches the truth for opening up the country. It is the foundation of the Japanese Empire, and has transformed Japan from 'The-Abundant-Reed-Plain' into 'The Land of Luxuriant-Rice-Fields.' After the country had been opened up, and the foundations laid by Shintoism, troubles arose that made other religions a necessity." He illustrates this by saying, "When a man is single he does not quarrel with his wife; when children are young, they do not dispute with their parents. But if a man is married, and has grown-up children, the five relations of Confucius and the teaching of Buddha become a necessity. So as life in Japan became more and more complex, Confucianism was useful in governing the country, and Buddhism in giving the people peace of mind. People are apt to think the original teaching was a great mistake, or that it was merely the invention of the Shinto priests, but they all contain great truth, and I intend to combine the good points of all three in 'Hotoku' and call it 'Shin-jiu-butsu-shomi-ichiriu-gan,' literally, a chemical compound containing the essence of Shintoism, Buddhism, and Confucianism. If we use this compound for the ills of our country, or its families, they will be cured. If we use it for debtors, their debts will be paid. If we use it for the diseases of profligacy, sloth, poverty, or luxury, all will be cured." His disciple, Hyodaiyu, who was at his side, asked him, "In

what proportion shall I mix these three teachings?" Ninomiya replied, "One spoon of Shintoism to one half of each of the other two." Some one near him drew a circle and divided it into quarters, assigning two of them to Shintoism and one to each of the other two. He then showed this figure to

Ninomiya and asked, "Is this what you mean?" He replied, "No, it is not. I said medicine. You cannot trace the various drugs in a chemical compound. They must be well mixed, for if given separately the people may be poisoned."

"Even if you study all the books of Shintoism, Confucianism, and Buddhism, and go to the extreme and become a hermit, you can never exceed the purpose for which these three religions exist; viz., to bring salvation to men. If you put any other object before you, you are led by false teaching. The true teaching of these religions is intended to save the world. Therefore, even if you become scholars, you must remember that the object of your scholarship must be to save the world. Otherwise you had better not be scholarly. You have no time to read any book that will not help you save the world. Life is short at the best, say sixty years, and when you deduct from this the time you spend in youth, old age, sickness, sleep, etc., life is truly short. We must not read useless books, nor spend our time on work that does not bring profit to ourselves and others."

Ninomiya once said to the famous priest Benzan, "The teachings of Buddhism are very voluminous; can you give me the gist of them in a word?" Benzan answered, "Avoid all evil, do all good." Ninomiya simply replied, "I understand."

Once on April the 8th, the anniversary of Buddha's death, Ninomiya went to a temple to see the annual ceremony of washing the statue of Buddha with tea made from boiled leaves. The statue has the right hand pointing to heaven, and the left pointing to the earth, as if to say, as Buddha said when he was born, "Between heaven and earth only I am noble." Seeing the statue, Ninomiya said to his disciples: "Even gamblers and freebooters use these very words. Buddha did not use them out of false pride, and these words must not be applied exclusively to him. The teaching ought to be that every one, thinking of himself, should feel that between heaven and earth there is no more noble man than he, for were he not existent there is nothing. Therefore every man is alone noble, and I may say more, even the hawk, the dog, or the cat is noble from his own standpoint."

"The teachings of Buddha are very interesting. They may be illustrated thus: the past life of a bean is the stalk, and the previous life of the stalk is a bean. We may say to the bean, 'You are the incarnation of the stalk. If you doubt it, I can refer you to a certain period in your past life when you were in a certain field, enduring storm, rain, wind, and cold as a stalk, until you finally became a bean. You must hasten and show your gratitude to your former existence by again becoming a stalk. This bean existence of yours is an illusion, but your future is very important.' Again we might say to the stalk : 'Your former existence was a seed. Your present existence has so many experiences, you must try to become a seed again. If you can only get past the present life, you can rest in peace in the storehouse.' This is like the teachings of Buddha."

"In Buddhism this life is transient, but the future is important. But we have our masters, parents, wives, and children here in this world, and even if we give these up, and separate ourselves from them, we have our bodies which have to be fed and clothed. Without money we cannot cross the ford or the sea. Therefore this world is important. Though Buddhism says that this world is temporary, it is like the famous saying of Saigyo,[1] 'If I think I am nothing because I have thrown myself away, yet I will feel cold on a snowy day.'"

"There are many plants that spring from seed, grow and produce blossoms and fruit, and then when the fruit falls off, the seed again germinates. This represents the law of revolving change (literally, ' circulation')."

"Buddhistic enlightenment is interesting, but it is injurious to humanity, because it lays bare the heart of humanity too plainly. If the roots of

[1] A priest who gave up his family and became a hermit.

grass are not hidden under the soil, they will die, so if the root of humanity is laid bare, humanity is injured, and human enterprise weakened. Confucianism does not expose the roots of the grass to the sun, but hides them in the soil and nourishes them. Confucianism is wise in this. A pine tree is always green, cherry blossoms are beautiful, and lotus flowers, pure. The roots of all such plants and trees are well hidden under the soil. The pawnbroker's shop will be enlarged at the expense of the poor, but should the root of his business be revealed, his trade would suffer. The magnificence of the daimio's castle depends on the retainers who are comparatively hidden." In this way, Ninomiya seems to imply that Buddhism, by dwelling too much on the past and future instead of the present, tries to explain human life so clearly that it really explains it away. He did not like Buddhism as well as Confucianism; the latter is more practical.

"The introduction of Buddhism into Japan was very difficult, but with modern Buddhism the case is very different. Ancient priests took their iron bowls, and obtained their living by begging. They[1] dressed in mean clothes, and were content to live in mountain caves or in the quiet of the forest; but modern priests are living in luxury. Dressed in

[1] Cf. Introduction.

costly clothes, they sit proudly in their magnificent temples, acting contrary to all the teachings of Buddha. This is not to be wondered at, for although they are forbidden to possess houses and lands, to hoard up treasures, or even to enter the society of the rich, the government has given them lands, the people have lavished on them treasures and goods, and even noble and rich are found among them. Just as in a great river the sand piles up where the water does not flow swiftly, so in somewhat the same way these abuses have accumulated in Buddhism."

"Taoism and Buddhism are very sublime, but they are of very little use to the people. Nikko and Hakone are very high mountains. The scenery is very beautiful, and the water is very pure, but people are not fed by mere scenery. My teaching is like the plain and the village. It is humble, with no magnificent scenery to look down upon; no clouds or water to admire, but various kinds of grain are produced which are the backbone of the country's wealth and prosperity. My teaching is practical. The wisdom of Buddhism is as pure as the sands of the seashore, but my teaching is as mud, out of which the beautiful lotus comes. The sublimity of the castle of the feudal lord depends on plains and villages. This truth is within reach, is humble, and is not lofty speculation. Practical virtue is also within your humble reach, and not beyond your depth. In this sense, even the humble and lowly are sublime and lofty."

Some one said to Ninomiya, "I have read that the great priest, Esshin Sozu, had said, 'If Buddhism, as taught by modern priests, were true, then Buddhism was harmful.' This was a very interesting confession." Ninomiya said: "This is true, but the same may be said of Confucianism and Shintoism. Confucianism as taught by modern teachers is not of much value; and Shintoism, although it is the great truth from the beginning of heaven and earth, gives out its charmed tablets to protect its members from danger. Besides this, true Shintoism tends to make the people rich, but modern priests are always poor. It is to be deplored that they do not know what true Shintoism is."

Some one who had visited Nikko said to Ninomiya: "In front of most temple grounds were signboards warning the people not to kill birds or animals on or about the sacred premises, but in Nikko I saw a notice to the effect that people were allowed to kill birds and animals in Nikko mountain, but not in any of the surrounding ones. That was a very curious sign-board." Ninomiya replied: "Buddhism makes a mistake in forbidding us to kill and eat birds and animals. It forgets that all things are living. All the food we eat is living, and without living food we could not subsist. About Nikko mountain, other living things are scarce, so Buddhism had to make a concession to the people in that vicinity, and permit them to eat animals and birds. Buddhism would be more correct in prohibiting the killing of living beings of the same order as man."

"Man, animals, and plants grow between heaven and earth, and are emanations of heaven. Wrigglers, flies, mosquitoes, plants, and trees are produced by the creative power of heaven, and not by any human effort. Of these, man is the head, the spirit of all, because when he disposes of any of these others, there is none to make objection, but man himself originally emanated from heaven. In Buddhism all men become Buddhas after death, but since our country is the land of the gods, we believe we become gods after death. Most people make the mistake of thinking this change occurs only after death. A man must be during his lifetime what he expects to be after death. It is as impossible for a mackerel to become a dried bonito after death, or for a pine tree to become a cedar tree when cut down, as it is for a man to become a god or a Buddha after death, if he is not one during his lifetime."

Some one asked Ninomiya what was the difference between retribution and the will of heaven. He replied: "The meaning of 'Ingwa' (retribution) is very clear. I explain it by this saying, 'If you sow rice, the rice plant will grow and blossom, and grain will appear.' So it is with society. Buddha looked at society from the standpoint of the seed, and therefore he used the word 'Ingwa.'[1] But if I sow seed, and it fails to get nourishment, it will not grow. It depends upon heaven and earth for growth, and from this standpoint Confucius emphasizes 'The will of heaven.' This is but a different way of looking at the same thing as Buddhistic retribution. When a wicked man had not yet his deserts, Buddha would say, his retribution was not yet ripe; while Confucius would say, the will of heaven had not yet come upon him. It is as if the seed were sown, but the fruit had not yet ripened. The expressions are different, but the fundamental idea is the same. It is a case of a man having to return what he has borrowed, or being compelled to do so by the help of the government. In this case the command of the government corresponds to the will of heaven."

Again Ninomiya was asked the meaning of "Innen" (relation in a previous state that determines the present). He said, "'In' is the seed,

[1] See note, page 9, Introduction.

and 'nen' is tilling and nourishing; combining these we get our harvest in Autumn."

In reply to the question as to whether there is a heaven or hell, he said: "According to Buddhism there is, but they cannot point to any one place and say this is heaven, or this is hell; according to Confucianism, which deals almost exclusively with the present, there is not, although nothing definite is said about it. I think that after death, and even in this present life, there are rewards and punishments for conduct. I think there are three existences, past, present, and future, and so I do not feel like denying the existence of heaven and hell. However, I would not say that we can get to heaven by merely repeating Nembutsu (Namu Amida butsu, the Buddhist prayer), or by donating money to a Buddhist temple. I say only that hell is the place of the wicked, and heaven the place of the good after death. Our going to heaven or hell does not depend on our relation to Buddhism."

"In Confucianism we read, 'Look not at what is contrary to propriety; listen not to what is contrary to propriety; speak not what is contrary to propriety; make no movement contrary to propriety' (Analects, 12, 2). This is very difficult for you common people to follow, so I will teach you that you must not see, hear, speak, or love, unless you are helping yourselves or others. If the sacred books do not help you and others, you need not obey them. Therefore it may be that my teaching is opposed to Buddhism, Confucianism, and Shintoism. Nevertheless, my teaching is true." His idea of his "Universe Book" gave him a good degree of assurance.

"Human life is like a waterwheel, half of which is in the water, and half out. As it revolves, one half goes with the stream, the other half against it. If you put it all under the water, or raise it all out of the water, it is useless. Buddhist hermits, who are the personification of wisdom, separate themselves from the world with its lusts and desires. They are like the waterwheel that is lifted out of the water. Common people who lack knowledge of duty, and who are moved only by lust and selfishness, are like the wheel sunk in the water. Neither of these is a useful element of society. Therefore the Confucian 'Mean' is important for human life."

"Confucianism teaches the law of circulation. Buddhism teaches transmigration. And to escape the tyranny of transmigration they teach Nirvana, the peaceful kingdom. Confucius teaches us to obey the will of heaven, and thus live a life of peace. My teaching is different, it is intended to enrich the poor, and give prosperity to those who need it. Escaping both the law of circulation, and transmigration, we may live in a place of prosperity. Fruit trees naturally bear well one year and rest the next. My idea is to prune and nurture them so they will bear well every year. It is natural for the rich to become poor, but I would overcome nature, and make prosperity permanent."

"As heaven and earth are one, so is truth one the world over. But there are many degrees in the knowledge of truth. All the different sects differ from one another more or less, because they are confined to very narrow limits. These limitations and barriers must be thrown down. The opinion of a man so hedged about by sectarianism is valueless, so far as I am concerned."

"There are many books which teach truth, but each has its own peculiar trend. There is no complete teaching. Buddha and Confucius were human, and their sacred writings are human. Therefore I look at the unwritten book of nature and compare their teachings with it. If they are not contradictory, I accept them. My opinion is always right. While the sun gives light, so long shall my teaching prevail without mistake."

CHAPTER IV

HUMAN VIRTUE AND NATURAL LAW

In an age when there is so much stress laid on naturalism and evolution, Ninomiya's opinion of the relation between human virtue and natural law[1] is of interest to us. We quote from the "Evening Addresses" and also from "Hotoku Ron," a book written by Ninomiya's son-in-law about the 29th of Meiji (circa 1897 A.D.). Some of these ideas remind us of Thomas Hobbes, as already pointed out by Dr. Kato in the Introduction. In one place we read that his son-in-law, Mr. Tomita, asked Ninomiya, "What do you mean by natural law and human virtue?" Ninomiya replied, "One originating principle prevails, by which Spring comes, and all things receive life; Summer heat, and all things grow; Autumn cool, and all things yield fruit; Winter cold, and all things are preserved. In this way the four seasons circulate wind, rain, snow, and frost in their proper seasons, year after year without change. This is nature, obeying which,

[1] Literally, Heaven's way, used by Mr. Tomita in the "Hotoku Ron" as synonymous with nature and natural law.

plants grow in Spring and Summer, and fade in
Autumn and Winter, and birds, animals, fish, and
worms follow after their daily food. If there is
much food, they have plenty; if not, they starve,
unable to help themselves. Living or dying, they
follow nature, nourishing only the physical. In
ancient times, men, like birds and animals, barely
existed physically. Animals and birds are provided
with means of protection and defence, and even
from birth are able to obtain food, and protect themselves from the cold and heat. The ancients were
not so provided for, and, being unable to eat many
kinds of fruit and roots, were constantly in a state
of starvation and suffering. Besides this, they
quarrelled over their food, and resorted to theft
and murder. Then sages appeared on the earth,
and, taking pity on man, established the 'Human
Way.' They taught the people to live quietly
together; to cultivate the soil; to plant the five
different kinds of grain; to build aqueducts,
dikes, and roads; to use farm implements; to
make furniture, and wear clothes; to live in houses
of wood and bamboo, instead of living in the open
air or in mountain caves. But as these only
satisfy the demands of the physical nature, the
sages established the moral law and taught the
people to obey it. In this way, for the first time, the
relation between father and son became congenial;

the relation between emperor and subject became righteous; the relation between husband and wife, distinct; the relation between elder brother and younger became one of respect; and between friends, became one of fidelity. In this way all men escaped the misery of their former existence, and became distinct from other animals. Every man wishing to live his life in peace must obey these five relations and follow nature. But this is a made way; if men neglect to obey these five relations they will quickly degenerate, their clothing will be torn, and lust will abound, fields will soon be deserted, aqueducts, dikes, and bridges will soon be broken. Deserted fields, broken dikes, torn clothes, and self-indulgence are all indications of the rule of nature. Rich soil, cultivated fields, well repaired dikes, good clothing, and the five relations, indicate the way of virtue. In short, the important point in connection with this human way is, to restrain selfish lust, and to follow economical principles, performing works of benevolence and righteousness. If you walk in the way of humanity, you will be saved from misery, but if you neglect or oppose this made way, you will degenerate into your former bird or animal existence."

"Human virtue differs from nature, being made by man. Natural law is seen in the growth of Spring, and in the decay of Autumn; in that fire burns, and water runs down hill; in that day and night revolve eternally without change. The success of human life depends upon our ability to plan and scheme. If we depend only on natural law, and are led astray by mere animal passion and lust, human life with all that is peculiar to it will be destroyed. Though there are no paths on the ocean, the ships have definite channels they must follow, or be dashed to pieces on the rocks. So, though it is natural for man to desire delicate food and extravagant clothing, he must control mere passion and lust, and live well within his means. This is the way of humanity. To sow our grain is natural, but if we wish to make the grain profitable, we pull up the weeds around it, to give it a better chance. It is not natural to pull up the weeds. So following natural desire, we must labor, but when natural desire clashes with duty, it must be restrained."

"The animal way, despised by everyone, is natural; the human way, revered by all, though not out of harmony with natural law, is a made way. The way of nature is to weather rain, sunshine and wind, to eat hay in Winter and fruit in Autumn, to eat greedily when there is plenty, without thinking of the future, and to starve when there is a famine. The way of humanity is to build storehouses, and provide rice for the four seasons, to wear clothes, and build houses for protection from the weather. The way of nature is unchangeable, but the way of humanity may be destroyed by idleness and neglect. It is a mistake for a man who is following the way of nature, to conclude that, because all things are going wrong, this is a very discouraging world. Human life is strenuous, and opposed to nature. The human way is to repair deserted places, and fertilize sterile plains. Few understand the difference between the human way and the way of nature."

"To-day is the winter solstice. The sun has reached its southern limit. By the will of heaven the nights are long. Even though we do not like the long nights and wish to shorten them, we cannot. This is heaven. By the will of heaven the saucer in this lamp is filled with oil. If the oil is not sufficient for the whole night, it cannot be helped. This is also the will of heaven. If I put in a smaller wick, the oil will last all night. This is where we must use human ingenuity. For example, Ise is the place where the Imperial shrines are situated. Men travel from Tokyo, over 200 miles, at a cost of about ten yen for twenty days, or an average of fifty sen per day. This is the will of heaven. If a man spends sixty sen a day, he will have a deficiency of two yen. If he spends only forty sen a day, he will have a surplus of two yen. In this way by human ingenuity, we can either lengthen or shorten the will of heaven. If we have no fuel this morning, and get some to-morrow, that is the will of heaven influenced by human effort. In the same way we can fill the empty tub (which is the will of heaven) by bringing water from the well. All things depend upon this law described in the old Japanese saying which is analogous to the saying, 'Heaven helps those who help themselves.' "

CHAPTER V

HUMAN DESTINY [1]

NINOMIYA's ideas on this subject were influenced by Buddhism, but he bases his thought on something more fundamental than Buddhist scripture. He was cosmopolitan enough to make truth universal, basing it on the essential nature of existence.

Speaking on this subject, Ninomiya said: "Common people often talk about chance or luck. They think that people are like pears or persimmons turned out of a box, and that it is a mere accident as to which comes to the top. They mistakenly think their position in the world is a matter of chance. If people are like persimmons or pears, their destiny is of little value, because it is not the result of their own effort. It is like gambling, and would be just as worthless. I shall teach you the true meaning of destiny. It is revolution toward

[1] The word I have translated destiny is "Un," which means literally, "circulation." This is suggestive of the Oriental idea of fate. The rich man becomes poor, and the poor man becomes rich, under circulating or revolving fate. The same word is used in "unchin," meaning freight, and in the phrase "Un ga yoi Hito," a lucky man.

a given point. 'Unten' (literally, 'heaven's luck,' or providence) was first revealed to man through the order and law manifested in the revolution of the planets. So, by the same order and law, if you do good to others, happiness will come to you, and if you do evil, misery will be sure to follow. It is said that a certain man would have been killed had his lantern not gone out by accident. Another was saved from disaster by the breaking of his sandal string. Of such things the common people say chance, luck, or accident, but I say there is always a causal relation, and a true destiny. Confucianism teaches that if we do good, good will follow; if evil, evil will follow. Buddhism is clearer, because it teaches us about the three worlds, past, present, and future. If we think of these three worlds, our destiny becomes clear. In this point Buddhism excels Confucianism. People should not be dissatisfied with the future world, because both happiness and misery are the direct result of our own conduct. For example, here is a blade of grass; in the past it was a seed, in the future it will become fruit or flower; so we see the meaning of the three worlds. It is not simply Buddhistic teaching, it is the truth at the very basis of the world, and prevailed before Buddha was born. We can read it in the unwritten sacred books of nature. I have a saying, 'Without voice or without savor, heaven and earth repeat over and over again the unwritten sacred books.' If you wish to read these books, you must close your physical eyes, and open the eyes of your soul. This truth prevailed from the beginning, not only in Japan, but in all countries of the world."

"In this life there are many accidents which must be provided against. If we have made proper provision, we will almost be able to say, there is no such thing as an accident, but if we have made no provision, then even a very slight accident may bring serious results. A certain sage said, 'Any country which had not provision made for at least three years cannot rightly be called a country.' I teach economy, not for its own sake, but that suitable provision may be made against accident. Some even criticise me, saying I am always saving, as though my chief purpose were to save. Those who understand my ideal will understand the difference between a miser and an economist."

CHAPTER VI

THRIFT [1]

THE best illustration of this teaching has already been given in connection with the redemption of the Soma estate. The following quotations will help to make the subject clear. Some one asked Ninomiya the question, "How would you undertake to accumulate inexhaustible wealth, in order to develop the soil and bring happiness to a people whose means are limited?" Ninomiya replied: "Whether the country be large or small, the area and the population are limited, but the wealth may be unlimited, if all human effort possible is made to labor, and economize, and save. Commonly, people count only the treasure before their eyes; we look into the future. Without 'Bundo' the expenditures of the country will be unrestricted, luxury will prevail, and money will be deficient. If there is a growing deficiency, money will have to be obtained from the lower classes, whose wealth is

---

[1] The word I have translated "thrift" is "Bundo." It is not quite equivalent to our word "thrift." The context will explain it. It is a technical word of the Hotoku Society.

very meagre. Extreme poverty follows, and they must dress in rags and eat poor food. They will not be able to support their children and their aged parents, so their homes will of necessity be broken up, and their fields deserted. The successful gardener carefully nourishes the roots of his trees and shrubs. The common people are the roots of the country, and the country, to be prosperous, must carefully nourish them, and decide upon its 'Bundo.' What is 'Bundo'? It is fixing all expenditure in proportion to the means of the people. How is this limit to be decided? Whether a country be rich or poor, it is the will of heaven. A sage has said, 'The superior man does what is proper in whatever position he is, whether it be a position of wealth and honor, or one of poverty; whether he be among barbarous tribes, or in sorrow and difficulty; wherever he is, he naturally does the proper thing.' Therefore in prosperity or poverty we must be content, and if in a state of decay, we must limit our expenditure. To strike a just average, we must reckon from the annual income of at least twenty or thirty years. Such limitation may cramp us, but we must patiently adhere to it if we would become prosperous and wealthy. In ancient times China and Japan did not borrow foreign money to open up their lands, but utilized only their own resources, and suc-

ceeded. So countries at present in a state of decay
do not need to borrow foreign money; if they will
only fix a limit to their expenditures, well within
their resources, they will soon have a surplus with
which to develop and cultivate their lands. So
in the early days of Japan, Amaterasu-O-Mikami
opened up this great reed-covered plain without
money. She depended only on the spade to cultivate the soil, and by saving part of the fruit for
seed each year, she gradually, year by year, opened
up more and more of the waste places. In the
same way we can open up any amount of deserted
plain, and rescue any number of people from
poverty."

"If the daimio should give up these economical
methods and live in luxury, his estate will in time
fall into decay, and his subjects be reduced to suffering. It would be as though the dikes were
broken and the country left open to deluge. The
daimio must persist in fixing his expenditure well
within his means, using the surplus for the good of
the common people."

In addition to recommending men to fix the limit
of their expenditures, Ninomiya exhorted men to
avoid luxury, and to exhort their descendants to
follow their example. In one case he says: "In
the teachings of Tokugawa Iyeyasu it is written,
'I, Tokugawa Iyeyasu, was born in a warlike time,

and was strictly taught the principle of revenge. But a famous Buddhist priest taught me the error of such a principle. He said we should rescue the people, and endeavor to make of them peaceful subjects, for this is the will of heaven. From that time I have followed his principle, and our descendants must do so forever, for it is fundamental to the best government of our country!'" Ninomiya quoted these words to a certain disciple, and added: "You must say to your descendants that you were very fond of luxury, and spent public money of the Tokugawa government, and your debt became so great, you all but lost your property. But by the method of 'Hotoku' you were saved from such disaster. You must forbid them to indulge in luxury, and bid them practise economy, giving one half of their income for public good. They must rescue the poor from poverty, and develop the resources of their villages. If they neglect these teachings, tell them you will disown them. If you teach them in this way they will be prosperous, just as Iyeyasu's descendants prospered for a long period because of his teaching."

Ninomiya gave a certain man this charm, as he was pleased to describe it. It was a saying, meaning, "All things except rice, soup and cotton clothes are only a trouble to their owners." He said the construction of the saying was poor, but the principle was important. He told the man to keep it, and when luxuries entered his home to look upon them as enemies. Even though it might be but a very little thing, it might prove to be the cause of his ruin.

He also warned men against going to excess in anything. To a certain man, who was in the habit of going to extremes in everything, Ninomiya gave this counsel: "All things have their limitation. Even in cooking there is a limit, without which the food will be overdone and uneatable. It is important to give advice, but advice given too often becomes interference, and is resented. Excess is as bad as neglect. Even plum blossoms if in excess become vulgar."

CHAPTER VII

"SELF-SACRIFICE" AND KINDRED SUBJECTS

NINOMIYA probably learned the meaning and value of self-sacrifice [1] by experience. In his boyhood we have seen him sacrificing much in order to help in the support of his brothers and sisters. It is said that he used to make straw sandals late into the night in order to buy wine for his sick father. We are also told that his father sacrificed much in order to help the more needy. All these early influences tended to impress on the boy's mind the value and the beauty of self-denial. In later years we have seen him recounting those early experiences and advising other men to give themselves to others. His teaching regarding self-sacrifice may be learned from the following quotations: —

[1] "Suijo" is the word I have translated self-sacrifice. It is a technical word of the Hotoku Society and is composed of two words, "Osu," to press down, and "Yuzuru," to give up, — the meaning being that one subdues himself and gives up either to another or for another time. The latter word has something of the force of our common expression, "In honor preferring one another."

"Without self-sacrifice human virtue cannot exist for even one day. Even the five relations, or the five virtues, cannot exist without it. Without it struggle, fighting, and quarrelling will arise. Self-sacrifice is characteristic of man, but struggle and theft is the conduct of beasts. In the beginning, before the existence of sages, human virtue did not exist. Man was scarcely different from the birds and animals. Amaterasu-O-Mikami was impelled by this virtue in opening up the great reed-covered plains, and bringing prosperity and happiness to the people. After that the people learned the five virtues, and the five relations, and became very different from the birds and animals. This principle applies to all countries between heaven and earth. Their peace, riches, and prosperity depend upon it. For example, if you have one bushel of rice and eat it, it will last only a few days, but if you sow it, it will produce many bushels, and if you continue to sow in increasing quantities each year, it will produce hundreds of bushels."

"Again, if a father denies himself for his child, we call it love. If a child denies itself for its father, we call it filial love. If an elder brother denies himself for his younger brother, we call it good. If a younger brother denies himself for his older brother, we call it harmonious relation. If a husband denies himself for his wife, we call it righteousness. If the wife denies herself for her husband, we call it obedience. Thus we see that if the family exercise this principle, they can enjoy prosperity. If Japan and her lords exercise it, the country will enjoy prosperity. If they follow the opposite principle, the country will decay. Again, I repeat, self-sacrifice is the foundation of all virtue, and of the five relations. Since I have understood this principle, I have tried to practise it for fifty years. By it I have raised many deserted villages, and rescued many poor people, so I speak from experience. The rich farmer or merchant does not have to work, but the poor man must labor for his living. The rich man is like a person at the top of a mountain, all things are at his feet. Therefore he becomes proud, falls into luxury, and finally destroys his family. My teaching of self-sacrifice will save a man from such folly and disaster. The sons of the rich who are not acquainted with it are in danger, and are not useful citizens.

"Bringing up children is like cultivating the soil. If the father fails to bring up good boys, he cannot get any recompense for his trouble, so he is not better off than the farmer who, after cultivating his fields, has his grain destroyed by a famine, and so reaps no reward. The loss in both cases is great. When I first came down to Sakuramachi, at the request of Lord Odawara, I succeeded in raising that district, but I did it at the cost of my own home. I sacrificed everything for that work. Buddha understood that the living must die, and that which is united must certainly be thrust asunder, therefore he separated himself from his family and his rich estate, and went forth to propagate his teaching. If a man is born, he must surely die. It makes little difference whether his life be long or short. If you light a long candle or a short one, it does not make much difference in the end, for both are consumed. Man must not forget that he must die sooner or later, and he should live every day as if it were his last, and value every day as if it were a treasure. If he lives a year, he has gained so much from heaven. Man of himself is nothing, and has nothing, but if he realizes that he has been given that treasure, life, he will value it very dearly for what he is able to accomplish. I have a saying, 'My body is borrowed, and I lend it to its previous owner, and I pray that the people may be peaceful and happy.' The former owner is heaven. We must not think our bodies are our own. We must be willing to sacrifice for the people, for our country, and for the world, and must pray that we may rescue even one man, one family, one village. This is the spirit of this saying, and of my whole life."

These quotations show us very clearly that Ninomiya valued unselfishness very highly. Mr. Uchi-mura in his short account of the sage tells of a village chief who had lost his influence with his people and who came to Ninomiya for advice. Ninomiya told him: "Selfishness is of beasts, and a selfish man is animal-like. You can have influence over your people only by giving yourself and your all to them." In reply to the question as to how to do this, Ninomiya said, "Sell your land, your house, your raiment, your all, and contribute the proceeds to the village fund, giving yourself wholly to the service of the people."

Ninomiya even offered to help the man if neces-sary, if he would give himself to the welfare of the public as outlined. We have already told the story of Magoyemon and his struggle with himself. Ninomiya thus exalted self-sacrifice and unself-ishness.

Ninomiya recognized that the greatest waste was that of the mind. Men who were living self-ish, useless lives were looked upon in somewhat the same way as he regarded the waste land. He wished men to be faithful and useful to the com-munity and worked, as he said, to restore the waste places in men's minds. The following quotation gives us his thought on this subject: —

"Our duty is to restore deserted places. Of these there are many kinds: fields deserted on account of debt; places where the soil is barren, and the taxes high; wealthy men living in luxury who are not useful to the country; men of talent and scholarship who have not learned to use these gifts for their country's benefit; men with healthy bodies living in idleness, gambling, and drinking; all such are waste places. Among these the waste and corruption of the mind is the greatest evil to the country. Waste of fields and mountains is secondary. But our duty is to cultivate all."

Ninomiya said: "The reason the country is not continuously prosperous is because each individual is seeking only his own interests. Rich men have no heart to save the world. They are avaricious and greedy, regardless of the blessings they receive from their country and from heaven. Poor men have the same spirit. They neglect to pay their taxes and their rent, or to repay borrowed money. Rich and poor alike neglect righteousness, and aim at unreasonable objects. Both alike are selfish. Therefore we should endeavor to correct these evil tendencies, and raise the people to better standards of life."

"Our income is the returning of what we give out. The farmer scatters manure, and prunes and nourishes his plants in the Spring, and in the Autumn he is rewarded by a good harvest. It does not do to eat vegetables as soon as they have sprouted, or to cut off limbs from newly planted trees. If a merchant seeks wealth without due regard for the buyer, he is not kind, and his store will not prosper. According to the old saying, 'Human lust (literally, "Human mind") is dangerous, and the moral mind is about to vanish.' We must polish the moral mind, and if we keep the proper mean, human life will be prolonged. If I covet too much for myself, heaven will take away what I have." [1]

"From the god-given soul in man comes the true heart, — our conscience; from the flesh comes the selfish heart, — the human mind. Bad grass growing in the fields must be taken out by the roots, or it will destroy the good plants. The selfish mind (literally, 'human mind') will hurt the true mind, therefore we must root out all selfishness, and nourish the virtues of charity, righteousness, propriety, and wisdom."

[1] Matt. 13 : 12.

CHAPTER VIII

DILIGENCE

NINOMIYA laid great stress on industry. Once when he was reforming a certain district his disciples said that the devil fled before industry and the Goddess of Happiness arose out of the soil in response to hard work. A few quotations will give us some idea of his thought on this important subject.

Ninomiya declared: "The spade and the sickle are important factors in the betterment of the country. They cannot be dispensed with for even one day. They changed Japan from the 'great reed-covered plains' of ancient times, into the 'rich rice-growing country' of modern times. The spade and the sickle, used industriously under the favor of heaven, will assure abundant crops of barley, rice, and other grains. Then money and treasure will accumulate, and our lives will be peaceful and happy. But we must not for a moment forget the importance of using the spade and the sickle." Ninomiya composed this saying, "Unlimited treasure piled up by the favor of the

Sun Goddess may be dug out by the spade, and reaped with the sickle." This saying is popular among the farmers, not for its style, but because of its sentiment.

"Work much, earn much, and spend little. Gather plenty of fuel, and burn as little as possible. This is the secret of making a country wealthy; it is not miserliness. Since human life is opposed to nature, we must save and provide for the future by industrious effort, the earnings of this year providing for the necessities of next year. Saving is the virtue of self-denial."

"If you wish to do great things, you must not despise the little things. Great things are the result of an accumulation of little things. For example, 1,000,000 koku of rice is composed of many grains of rice. When you cultivate many acres of land, you do so spadeful by spadeful. When you walk twenty-five miles, you do so step by step. If you build a great mound, you do so basketful by basketful. In the same way, by being diligent in little things you may accomplish much."

"A true gentleman[1] does not think about living an easy life. His ideal is not merely to live and eat. He rather puts forth his effort on good works, avoids useless words, and studies truth from men

[1] Sometimes translated, "the superior man."

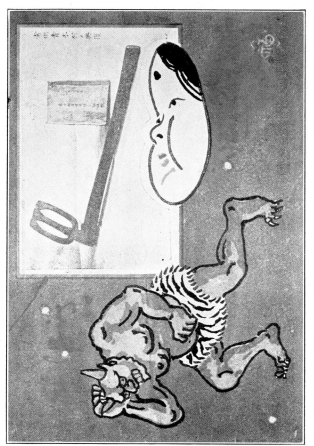

THE FACE OF THE GODDESS OF HAPPINESS APPEARING AND THE DEVIL FLEEING FROM IN-
DUSTRY, REPRESENTED BY THE HOE.

and from experience. Some expected Confucius to praise such men, but he merely said they were truly fond of learning. This, in short, means that to abstain from wine, to work with diligence, to avoid useless things, is a man's simple duty, and not a thing to elicit praise."

One of Ninomiya's disciples liked to sing: "In the lion mask,[1] the man who walks behind has no anxiety. He does not play the flute, he does not beat the drum, he does not guide the mask. Serving merely as the hind legs of the lion, he follows without care." When Ninomiya heard him, he told him such sentiment was unbecoming. Only a man of talent, who has accomplished a great work and then retired, may indulge such sentiment. Ordinary men need the spirit to work, and to do whatever lies in their power to do, though it may not be any great work. We receive education from our fathers and our teachers, then we in turn must become the teachers of our own children and younger brothers. We receive kindness from our neighbors, and in our turn pass some kindness on to others. This illustrates a great truth of human life which this song tends to destroy. If there were no one to act as fore legs, you could not act as hind legs. The officials of the country, by their work, enable you to lead a peaceful life. Con-

[1] A popular amusement at New Year's.

sidering all these blessings, to sing this song is very wrong." Ninomiya changed it thus, "Since there are men to play the flute, and beat the drum, and dancers to dance, even I, ignorant as I am, may act as the hind legs."

"The rich and the poor are not so far separated. Whether a man is rich or poor depends on his mental attitude. The poor man works for yesterday or last year, so that however hard he may work, he meets with no success. The rich man works for the present, or for next year, and is successful. When poor people have no wine, they borrow money from their neighbors and drink. If they have no rice, they borrow and eat. This is a cause of much poverty. The way to live a peaceful life is to carry faggots from the mountain to-day to boil to-morrow's rice, and this evening to make hay rope to mend the fence to-morrow. If a poor man wishes to cut weeds, and has no sickle, instead of borrowing from his neighbor, let him seek work and earn money to buy one. This is the secret of wealth, the way of the Imperial ancestral gods, who, alighting upon this great reed-covered plain, established ancient Japan."

In addition to diligence, Ninomiya advised men to take time by the forelock, and plan for the future. In one place he says: "Decision and care are very important. Without them success is impossible, even in small matters. There are twelve months in the year, but rice only ripens at the beginning of winter. This is a fixed law, so farmers act in accordance with it. If it were thought that rice would ripen only once in every two or three years, people would be satisfied with that, and adjust themselves to that law. If there is a deficiency in our living, the lack is in ourselves. The end of the year does not come suddenly, but though men know of its coming, they do not give proper heed to it."

CHAPTER IX

TRUE LEARNING

FOR Ninomiya, learning was practical. He encouraged young men to get learning if they intended to come home and improve their family name by hard work. In his "Evening Addresses" he says: "True learning does not consist in books, it must be practical and capable of practical application. In the Analects we read: 'Virtuous manners constitute the excellence of a neighborhood. If a man selecting a residence does not select one where such influences prevail, how can he be wise?'" Commenting on this, Ninomiya said: "By the influence of environment our characters are changed. If we do not select a good place in which to live, we are foolish. This is true, but pilgrims and tenants cannot live in good places freely because they cannot select their place of residence. He who has fields, houses, or mountains cannot readily remove them from bad environment, and according to this teaching he is foolish. I think a man is unwise to remove from his own village, for, as I said before, we must apply our learning in a practical way. To remove is expensive. It would be better for the man to reform himself, and then reform his environment, endeavoring to change the moral standard of the village. It is not so impossible to reform a bad village. First, conduct yourself according to truth, then, beginning in your own family, reach out after the villagers one by one. Following the teachings of Confucius, praise the worthy, and do not punish the bad. Praise the good, and help the bad for five years, and the village will be reformed. Many scholars do not know how to read and apply truth to advantage. They blame the villagers for the evil conditions of the village, and endeavor to thrust out the bad men. At the same time they do not try to mend their own conduct. The reformer must act with sincerity."

"Men of ability are generally lacking in morals. Such persons like the teachings of Shinkwan.[1] Those who cannot read, admire Sangokushi and Taikoki, the former being the history of wild Chinese heroes, the latter, that of Hideyoshi. The former resemble modern freebooters and dislike books, such as 'The Mean' and 'The Analects' because they cannot understand moral principles. Moral principles are not grasped merely by intelli-

---

[1] This teaching is said to resemble modern socialism, and was forbidden in the Tokugawa period.

gence. Young men especially are attracted by wild stories such as those of Shinkwan, but they are very harmful, because they present evil in too attractive a form."

Rikiyu, a teacher of ceremonial tea, in the employ of Hideyoshi, wrote this saying, "Though the tea-dipper goes from cold to hot (literally, 'hell'), since it has no mind, it has no suffering." Ninomiya considered the saying deficient, because it suggests annihilating the mind as if that were important. To destroy mind is to wrong the country, for a man's mind is his real self. So he amended the saying thus, "If we have our hearts fixed as a dipper, we will not feel any suffering though we pass from hot to cold."

Ninomiya said: " There are four great laws governing the relations between heaven and earth, parent and son, husband and wife, the farmer and his plants. If we follow these laws there will be no mistake. I have a saying, 'If I follow the law of love to my boy, I will obtain the truth, even though I do not study it.' This expresses the spirit of the four laws. Heaven and earth together feed all creatures. Parents feed their children and rejoice in their development, and the children love their parents in return. Husband and wife beget children. Farmers toil, and plants and grain grow. In every case both of the related parts enjoy the relation. The merchant must follow the same law if he would be successful. Both buyer and seller must rejoice in their relation to each other. If only the seller rejoices, it is not true trading. I endeavor to follow these laws in my own work and teachings."

Bidding farewell to Iidaka Rokuzoo of Uraga, who was an inveterate gossip, Ninomiya gave him this advice: "When you return to your native country, do not speak your mind to others, but set your mind to teach itself. The mind that teaches is moral, the mind that is taught is human. You must teach your mind at all times. If you drink wine, teach your mind not to drink to excess. If it obeys, it is well; if not, continue your teaching until it does. If your mind tends to luxury, you must teach it economy. After your mind has learned perfect obedience, and responds to your will, then you may begin to teach others, and not till then. I suppose you intend to become a merchant. That is good, but you must not think only of gaining wealth. Learn the true way of merchants and walk in it; forgetting this, you will fail. Walking in the true way, you will be industrious, and your business will prosper."

"To know the truth of heaven and earth, we must study the unwritten sacred book of nature. To read this book we must use the eyes of the mind, not the eyes of the body. The physical sight is limited, but that of the mind is unlimited." His disciple Oshima, on hearing this teaching, said: "Your teaching is very profound, and I have been so impolite as to compose a saying describing it: 'If we close our eyes, and look well at the world we can see the bright, shining morning moon, even on the last evening of the year.'" Notice that according to the old lunar calendar there would be no moon at the end of the month. Ninomiya praised the saying.

A disciple brought him a copy of the following poem from the flag of Kusunoki Masashige, an ancient hero famous for his loyalty to the Emperor: —

> "Injustice cannot overpower reason:
> Reason cannot overpower law,
> Law cannot overpower authority,
> Authority cannot overpower heaven,
> Heaven is just and impartial."

"A great truth is expressed in these lines. However much power a man may have he cannot overpower heaven. We cannot depend upon reason, for it is sometimes subdued by authority. Law stands, even though reason be suppressed. We cannot subject law to authority, but heaven exists above all. It is written in a popular old song, 'We can travel by horse the eight ri (twenty miles) across Hakone mountain, but we cannot pass the Oi river by any means.' So we can conquer man by intellect, eloquence, or authority, but we cannot subdue heaven. This is called in Buddhism, Mumonkwan (No-gate-barrier). The Hei family, the Gen family, the Ota family, and the Toyotomi family were destroyed by opposing heaven. Covetous men wish to extend their property by illegitimate methods, but heaven interposes, and they fail."

CHAPTER X

THE PROBLEM OF EVIL

NINOMIYA's view of Good and Evil was not unnatural when we consider his view of "The Way." When he affirms that all things come from "One Originating Spirit," we expect him, like Ito Jinsai, to hold that "The Way" is natural. On the contrary, he maintains with Ogiu Sorai, that "The Way" is made. When "The Way" is made by man, good and evil are of necessity merely relative. Motoori went to the opposite extreme in making the way, "The way of the gods," above nature and human learning. These various views are strikingly similar to the views expressed by Western ethical and religious thinkers. However, a few quotations from his teachings will enable us to appreciate the position the sage took on this subject, and if we really understand his position we cannot but admire the original way he expresses himself. The substance of his thought is as follows: "The problem of good and evil is a very difficult one. It is a mistake to talk of the origin of good and evil, for there is none. The difference between good and evil arises from man. If there were no men, there would be no good or evil. Let me illustrate. Man thinks it good to cultivate waste places, and bad to neglect them, but the bear and the deer think waste places very good. The thief thinks it good to steal, but the law pronounces it an evil. We cannot discern clearly what is good and what is evil. It is like saying far and near. Suppose you put up two stakes, one marked far, and the other, near. Your position decides which is far and which is near. I have this saying: 'If you look far enough, there is no difference between far and near. The difference depends only on your standpoint.' In the same way there is no good and evil. When they are closely connected with human interests, man often mistakes the one for the other. But if he looks from a distance, with a disinterested eye, he can distinguish them. To judge whether a building is plumb, we must look from a distance. To judge truly of anything, whether it be good or evil, we must not be too closely connected with it. If a man says Tokyo is far, he is probably a man from Kyoto; if a man says Osaka is far, he is probably a man from Tokyo. So there is no absolute difference between loss and gain, good and evil, calamity and happiness; it is simply a difference of standpoint. There is nothing absolutely good or absolutely evil."

243

"When a man is born, people rejoice, but even then his death is assured. When a flower blooms, it will certainly fade away in a few days. In the Nehankyo, a sacred book of Buddhism, there is a good illustration. A very graceful and beautiful woman entered a certain man's house. The host inquired who she was. She replied, 'I am Kudokutan, the Goddess of Happiness. Everywhere I go I bring unlimited joy.' The host rejoiced at this, and invited her to remain. Then the goddess said: 'I have one female attendant, who will come presently, please invite her also to remain with me.' The host gladly agreed to this. When she came she was very ugly, so he asked her who she was. She replied, 'I am Kokuan Ten, Goddess of Misery.' The host was indignant and ordered her to leave at once. She replied: 'Kudokutan is my elder sister, I cannot separate myself from her, even for a little while. If you keep her, you must keep me also. If you order me away, you must send her away also.' The host decided to send both away. This illustrates how, in human life, happiness and misery go hand in hand. They are not two, but one in origin. For example, if I cut eggplants or radishes with a large cooking knife, that is happiness; but if I cut my finger, it is misery. The difference is in the way in which the knife is held. So the difference between happiness and misery is not absolute, but relative, depending upon the individual.''

"If you make aqueducts and build dikes, water is useful as a means of irrigation, but if uncontrolled, and allowed to flood the fields, it will wash the nourishment out of the soil, and leave the fields in a deserted condition. It is the same water, but in one case it brings happiness, and in the other misery. So wealth, if used only for selfish purposes, is a source of misery, but if used for the good of society, it will be a source of happiness. The same principle applies to any treasure."

"All happy and sad events, tribulations, joy, and all such experiences, are not absolute, but relative. When a cat catches a rat, there is joy for the cat, but misery for the rat. When a snake swallows a frog, it is joy for the snake, but misery for the frog. The joy of the hawk is the misery of the sparrow; the pleasure of the hunter is the discomfort of the birds and animals. All the world is the same; some rejoice over victory, or the acquisition of wealth, while others are mourning because of failure and loss. Certain Buddhists despise the world and retire to some solitary mountain, where they forfeit every opportunity of usefulness. Their spirit may be good, but their method is bad. Our method is good, because we make others to rejoice with us."

"From a good origin, good results spring, from a bad origin, bad results. Every one knows this, but since the results are sometimes slow in coming, we forget the principle. A country's peace or unrest, a family's prosperity or decay, a person's misery or happiness, all depend on this same principle."

"It is a mistake to lay the responsibility of a deserted village on the people's idleness,[1] for this is not the only cause. Every man desires wealth and prosperity for his own village and home. One of the great causes of waste places lies in the fact that the taxes are high, and the attitude of the government unsympathetic. The government must look after the rice boxes of the people."

[1] Literally, "idle farmers." Farmers live in villages in Japan.

CHAPTER XI

SINCERITY [1]

In the life of Ninomiya we have seen him giving to the old root-digger about seventy-five dollars because he felt that his heart was right and that his sincerity of motive would have a good moral effect on the other men. He believed and used to say: "One man is a very small thing in the universe, but his sincerity can move heaven and earth. Sincerity alone can turn misery into happiness." He constantly emphasized sincerity and practical virtue. He valued them more than eloquence and ability because they were able to govern not only man, but birds, animals, grasses, and trees.

He said: "Eloquence and ability have their places among men, but they do not apply to birds and animals. Birds and animals may be deceived, but grass and trees never. Though a man be more clever than Komei, a wise man of China, he cannot make grass and trees to prosper. The greatest learning and wisdom are useless without sincerity and practice. Therefore we admire these traits."

[1] This means the true heart and deals with the honest and truthful rather than with what we would popularly call "sincerity."

Ninomiya did not sanction insincerity even in jest, as the following incident shows. One of Ninomiya's disciples was an inveterate gossip, and, moreover, did not like to rectify mistakes. Ninomiya told him every one was liable to make mistakes, and when the mistake was discovered, the wise man reflected upon it, and endeavored to rectify it. This man not only failed to reflect upon his mistakes, but tried to conceal them, by pretending to be better than he was. This was not heroism, and no true gentleman admired such behavior. "All young people make mistakes which should be corrected at once. One should not lie, even in jest, for from lying, great evils may arise. An ancient sage once said, 'Calamity comes from the mouth.' To slander another is not good, even though the reviling words may be true. It is not good to publish another's evil, or to magnify it from the size of a needle to the size of a stick. It is good to praise, but not to an extreme. It is not wise to inform others of your own good qualities. Do not unnecessarily say things to displease people; such words are seeds of discord."

He believed in being true in heart even under most trying circumstances. Perhaps no one's lot can be harder than that of the daughter-in-law, who is married into her husband's ancestral home. Speaking of this, he says: "People like a luxurious

and easy life, and dislike hardship and trial. When
a young bride goes to her husband's home, in summer she feels like a person sitting on the mats of a
burning house; in winter she feels as if she were
standing out in a cold field. But she is very happy
when she brings her husband to her father's home;
in summer she feels like one in the refreshing cool
of an ice house; in winter, like one who draws near
to a burning house. But in any case she must feel
that she has a divine call, and that she must obey
that call, and accept her adopted home as her true
home. She may have to endure suffering, but she
must not swerve from the path of duty, but remain
as firm as Fudo san.[1] If she has a true heart, she
will work with all her might, as the farmer works
in heat or cold, and as the samurai endures the
hardships of the battle-field."

In a little Japanese periodical called "The Yama-
to-Damashii" (The Spirit of Japan), a writer on
Ninomiya quotes from his "Evening Addresses"
two very excellent passages on sincerity, to the
effect that sincerity may be known without instruction or study. We do not need books or
teachers to learn sincerity. Its path lies in such
everyday experience as eating when we are hungry,
sleeping when tired, and rising when we waken.
He illustrates this by an old saying, "The water

[1] See note, page 100.

fowls, when they come and go, leave no path behind them and yet they do not forget the way." He further says: "Unless[1] the path is clear without records or books, and without requiring study or instruction, it is not the path of sincerity. Our teaching does not set value on books. We make the universe our sutra. In this sutra, daily repeated to us, lies the path of sincerity. We reject the views of those scholars who set aside this precious sutra of the universe and seek for the path in books. We should with our eyes wide open look at the sutra of the universe and there seek for the path of sincerity. Heaven is silent, and yet the seasons come and go, and all things produce their fruit; and by its unwritten sutra and unspoken teachings rice grows when it is sown and wheat bears ears when its seeds are scattered; relying upon the path of sincerity for the same unchanging reason we should do our best to follow with our whole heart."

[1] Cf. "Spirit of Japan," April, 1910, No. 4.

PART III

AN ESTIMATE OF HIS TEACHINGS

CHAPTER I

CONTRAST Ninomiya's humble birth with the great work he accomplished in an age when there was no freedom, no people's rights, and when class distinction was so strong that Raisanyo the historian could say, "Even excellent men cannot stretch out their feet," and we must frankly recognize that Ninomiya deserves a place not only among great Japanese, but among great men of his age anywhere. We admire his original way of saying things that were not in themselves original. He is in this respect a typical Japanese. A Japanese gentleman, hearing the criticism that Japanese lack originality, replied, "If you mean by that, that we lack causative originality, there is some truth in it, but we do not lack adaptive and additive originality." Ninomiya possessed "adaptive and additive" originality. He could apply old truths to circumstances that were new. In this respect, even though he claimed to be "only a farmer," he was a very highly educated man.

His problem was essentially an economic one. His mind was first directed to this problem by his effort to redeem his father's estate. His successful accomplishment of this comparatively easy task led to his being called in to redeem the estate of Hattori. This having been well done, he was called in to assist the lord of Odawara in the redemption of Sakuramachi. On the death of Lord Odawara he was employed by the government to help solve some of the economic problems of the day. Thus naturally his great mission was to redeem waste land and restore deserted villages. The importance of this work will be understood by reviewing the conditions of his time as outlined in the introduction.

In accomplishing this work, his method of "Bundo" was a very ingenious one. In some ways it resembles the Western custom of laying aside a proportion of one's income for purposes of charity and benevolence. It is a great thing to see a man systematically lay aside a portion of his income for redeeming lost estates and helping the poor. He learned this method by experience. He learned the value of money by cultivating a small tract of waste land in order to buy oil to carry on his studies.

His method of helping the poor of society is admirable. Western socialists who are grappling with the same problem with which Ninomiya grappled might well sit at his feet and learn. Their desire to do away with governments and capital is the result of a questionable attitude toward society, and might easily give rise to greater problems than it is intended to solve. Ninomiya's method, instead of levelling down, is one that ought to have a tendency to lift up and draw out the best that is in the man who is down. Let the men who through ability, tact, and industry have risen to well-earned positions hold their position. Were they to organize in a systematic way to help other men who are worthy and industrious, much of the ill feeling against them would vanish and a better social condition would result.

By the application of his methods in the age and under the conditions in which he worked, he was able usually to carry out his economic programme. In case conditions were not favorable to his plan, as, for example, in the redemption of the Soma estate, he was wise enough to refuse even to attempt to put his method into operation.

CHAPTER II

HIS VALUE OF THE MORAL

In attempting to reform the economic conditions of his times, he was quick to perceive the value of the moral as well as the religious.

When he was called upon to redeem the waste land of Sakuramachi, he refused to accept money for the task, because money was bad for the morals of the people. In regard to the work around Lake Imbra, his report, that without an improvement in the moral condition of the people wealth would only hasten their destruction, shows the value he placed on the moral.

This is also shown in his attitude to the old man who spent his time digging stumps. He saw the moral value of the man's evident sincerity and rewarded it, even though the man was unable to do as much work in a day as some of the others. The other man who appeared to be doing so much was severely reprimanded before his fellows for insincerity and scheming. The value Ninomiya puts on sincerity or truthfulness is one of his strongest points. It is largely the result of Confucian teaching. The Japanese have some very famous sayings that indicate that truthfulness has always been valued by them. An old proverb says, "God dwells in the honest head." Sugawara Michizane (847–903 A.D.), a famous scholar who is sometimes worshipped as the God of Learning, has a saying that "if true in heart, God will bless you even if you do not ask Him." The short poems or sayings of the present Emperor contain similar ideas. "If man is not ashamed before God, then his heart is true," and "If you have a true heart, God will constantly communicate with you." When his country was forced to go to war with Russia, he wrote this, expressing the sincerity he felt: "We have tried to be sincere in word and deed and have exhausted every means to state a clear and truthful case, but all in vain. Now may the God who sees the hearts of men approve of what we do." The Empress in a poem translated by Professor Lloyd of the Imperial University also recognized the same idea:—

> "Take heed unto thyself; the mighty God,
> That is the soul of nature, sees the good
> And bad that man in his most secret heart
> Thinks by himself, and brings it to the light."

From these quotations we see that Ninomiya was giving expression to one of the most worthy elements in Japanese thought and character.

With his teachings about self-sacrifice, industry,

and diligence no one can find fault. When he advises men to give themselves to others and, without considering themselves, to work for the redemption of society by saving man after man, home after home, village after village until all Japan having been uplifted, the work should extend all over the world, his teaching is in harmony with one of the highest ideals of Christianity.

His expressions regarding evil have a natural reference to his great problem, and consequently have a more evident bearing on what we might call economic evils than on evil in general. He is right in maintaining that the distinction of good and evil is correlative, as, for example, his own illustration "far and near," to which we may add inner and outer, cause and effect, etc.

If he meant to indorse entirely the illustration from Buddhism in regard to happiness and misery, then he leaves himself open to the charge of pessimism so prevalent in the Orient. We cannot say that happiness and misery are of necessity so united together that because a man is happy to-day he must be unhappy to-morrow. Much less can we say that because one man is happy, another must be unhappy. It is true, as Ninomiya has pointed out, that the same event in different settings might bring happiness one time or misery another; might bring happiness to one man and misery to another.

The agreeable and disagreeable are elementary facts of experience, and there is no reason why one demands the other. However, the interpretation of an agreeable sensation may make a man happy, or it may make him wretched. To use a very homely but apt illustration: A man picks up some soft, wet object in the dark. If, interpreting his sensation, he says to himself, "This is that pure soap that I misplaced the other day," he is conscious of nothing but pleasure. But if, interpreting the same agreeable sensation, he says to himself, "This is some decayed vegetable matter that the cook has carelessly dropped," he has a wretched experience. What was practically the same sensation brings joy on the one hand and wretchedness on the other. Ninomiya was right in making good and evil, joy and misery, depend on one's attitude and consequent interpretation, but wrong, in so far as his discussion would seem to make the agreeable and disagreeable feelings, logical correlatives rather than elementary given facts of experience. Ninomiya distinguished between the natural way, as manifested in the laws of nature, and the human way, as manifested in the institutions and virtues of man. He gives the human way, which he calls "A Made Way," a higher place than the natural way. It is interesting to note that Professor Huxley recognized the ethical struggle, but called it artificial and unnatural; that Nietzsche elevated what he called the natural way and belittled the so-called ethical. The cynics made the same distinction as Ninomiya, but they held that the social order (Ninomiya's human way) was lower than the natural order (Ninomiya's natural way) just because it was a made way, and therefore artificial. Both agree that if the made way be abandoned, man would become like the birds and beasts. We would not attempt to do anything but support Ninomiya's position, and yet this can only be done by assuming that the made way, whether made by the sages or prophets, by the gods or God, is the expression of certain inherent conditions and needs of man. It is therefore just as *natural* for man as nature's way is for nature.

CHAPTER III

HIS APPEAL TO RELIGION

WHEN Ninomiya attempted to improve the moral condition of the people, he found that moral suasion alone was powerless to accomplish his ends. Excellent as his teaching was, he felt that Sakuramachi was not responding to his efforts. This led him to turn to religion. He suddenly left his work and ceased teaching and spent nearly three weeks in earnest fasting and prayer before the idol of Narita. Here he received great inspiration. His prayer was answered. The people rallied around him, and as a result a complete change took place in the conditions of the country around Sakuramachi. When famine broke out a few years later, he was able to open up his stores and not only feed the people of his master's estate, but was able to help the neighboring estate in which the people were suffering.

Ninomiya gives us a key to interpret idol worship in Japan. He pointed to the god "Fudo Myo" and said to his disciples, "Without such a spirit you are useless." A Buddhist priest in a sermon gave an illustration that gives us some light on the nature of their idol. A band of soldiers was arrested and thrown into prison by the Tokugawa government in the stormy times immediately preceding the revolution of 1868. They became very angry, especially as they thought they were treated unjustly. When the jailer was passing in food through the little window of their cell, they seized his hand and maltreated it. In their company was one boy who was very quiet, dignified, and obedient. It was noticed that every morning and evening he took out two little dolls and, placing them before him, reverently greeted them, saying, "Good morning, Mother," "Good morning, Father." At mealtime he again bowed before them and expressed the gratitude he felt to his parents for the food he ate. This was repeated so often that the others began to respect him for his filial piety and connected his constant good conduct with the influence of these dolls, which were used to keep his parents ever before his mind. Commenting on this incident, the Buddhist preacher said,[1] "We need dolls to act as flying machines to enable our hearts to soar to the place where dwells the true father of us all, to the presence of the Hotoke.[2] We need not trouble ourselves about the material used in making these images. Half an inch of decayed

[1] Cf. "The Praises of Amida," by Professor A. Lloyd, M.A.
[2] Buddha.

Fudo-Myo, a Japanese God, unmoved in the Midst of Fire.

wood, a sheet of old paper, a lump of clay, a block of metal, anything will do so long as it is a symbolical representation and prevents our forgetful hearts from becoming oblivious of the Tathagata.[1]   Before these symbols we bow down, and in doing so our hearts are lifted up in thought to the great heart of the Tathagata."

These idols, then, are similar to the use of the crucifix and images in Roman Catholicism.   Just as we begin to teach a child, using the balls, blocks, and other objects of the kindergarten, so the idol is an object used to keep before the mind some invisible truth or principle that otherwise the primitive man could scarcely grasp.   So long as we use pins or badges as signs of our allegiance to certain societies or principles we cannot be severe on the idol worshipper.   The idol represents the kindergarten stage of religion and perhaps has had just as important a place in the religious education of the race as the picture has had in the education of a child.   Even the Jews connected religious worship with certain objects and places, but Jesus Christ gave a more highly developed idea of worship when He said, "The hour cometh and now is when the true worshipper shall worship the Father in spirit and in truth."[2]

We admire the liberal attitude of Ninomiya to

[1] Amida Buddha.   [2] John 4: 21.

the older religions of Japan. Too many of us take the attitude that the study of comparative religions is interesting, but that Christianity is not one of them. Ninomiya had a broader conception of religion than this. He said, "The Way is one," and his thought concerning the universe implies that religion is one. This subject introduced by Ninomiya is one of great complexity. If the Way is one, and if religion is one, the purification of its highest manifestations in the world by science and education should finally lead the East and West together. Of course the fact that all of the great religions are so broken up into sects would indicate that that time is far-distant, and yet it does seem that all that is required to bring Northern Brahminism, Northern Buddhism, Confucianism, and Western Christianity together is time, education, and devotion to Truth. They are all working on essentially the same problems and with many somewhat similar instruments.

In making the universe his teacher, Ninomiya rises above most great teachers of the Orient. Our only regret is that he did not give this a greater place in his thought. The idea makes one feel that here, as in his estimate of the individual, he has been influenced by Western thought.

The teachings of "Hotoku" are not altogether original with Ninomiya. Kaibara Ekiken says:

"We have received great blessing from heaven, even more than others. How can we make return to heaven for all we have received?" This is the basis of Japanese filial piety and loyalty. A Japanese student, if asked the reason for his filial piety and loyalty, will invariably answer, "We must love our parents and our Emperor because of the blessings they have bestowed upon us." Other scholars like Hirata gave reasons why man should give gratitude to the gods and to their ancestors. Ninomiya had an original way of appealing to this spirit, to rouse the farmers and working men of his day to industry. The "Hotoku" Society itself resembled movements inaugurated by Matsudaira Sadanobu and Miura Baien. Some similarity may also be found in the movement among the merchant classes known as "Shingakusha," founded by Ishida Baigan. Ninomiya, however, succeeded in so incorporating into the fundamental principles of his society the three most popular ideas in Japan to-day, viz. patriotism, morality, and industry, that while the other organizations are comparatively unknown, the society of "Hotoku" is steadily gaining in power and influence.

Ninomiya's ethics is based on the appeal to make returns to heaven, earth, and man for their blessings. In order to see all that is involved in this as a basis for ethics, we must distinguish between gratitude to the godlike ancestors on the one hand and gratitude to earth and heaven on the other. In the first case we can understand how a living influence could be obtained by an appeal to be grateful to our parents or ancestry. But it is not an appeal on which we can base a whole system of ethics. It is too narrow. It was suitable to Japan closed up to herself in which she was practically a family, with the Imperial family as her head, but it is not sufficient as a basis for universal truth and world-wide commerce and industry. Some broader and more cosmopolitan view is necessary in order to be successful in world-wide intercourse. For example, Ninomiya recognized the necessity of both buyer and seller being satisfied in a bargain. This principle is obeyed in Japan between Japanese, where a spirit of brotherhood exists, but for some reason their reputation in world-wide commerce is different. It is probably because they need a wider view of human brotherhood. This must be based on something more far-reaching and universal than the Emperor or his ancestors, although both he and they should always hold a most important place in the mind of every loyal Japanese.

Even in Japan, however, this basis for ethics has proven too narrow, as is shown by the recent, much-to-be-deplored anarchist plot. Such men as nihilists and anarchists, if consistent, do not feel respect for their ancestry. But not only that, they feel rather that their ancestry have left social and economic problems for them to solve, and, consequently, there is for them no power in an appeal to be grateful to their ancestors. Some wider and more universal basis for ethics must be established in order to safeguard the nation.

On the other hand, in so far as "heaven and earth" are not personified, but are regarded as physical in their constitution, it is difficult to see how any living inspiration can be received from them, or how we can recognize blessings received from them as due to anything but the operation of what is called natural law. Return to such a natural law could only be made by recognizing and fully taking advantage of it to further improve the conditions of life; for a law of nature really established can obviously not be disobeyed.

CHAPTER IV

SUMMARY

NINOMIYA claimed that his "medicine tablet" was calculated to cure all the ills of the people, including poverty, luxury, and immorality. His teaching was intended to develop all kinds of waste places, among which he placed the corruption and waste of the mind as the greatest evil in the country. He used to say, "If we would only develop the deserted wastes in human minds we could then let deserted fields look out for themselves." When appointed to his last great work, he expressed his regret that instead of being appointed to refine human minds he was again appointed to restore deserted places. In teaching Magoyemon, the rich miser, we see that even as a moral teacher Ninomiya had a good degree of success. But as a matter of fact, however, his great successes lay in helping men in their economic struggle. His "medicine tablet" did not always meet with the same success when administered to immorality. In Sakuramachi we see him bringing in young men and training them, leaving the older men like old plants to die out. We cannot but sympathize with the standpoint he took, for there is no doubt that once a man has become old in immorality and evil habit his hope for reformation has become small.

This brings before us a problem of evil that, because of Ninomiya's call to solve the economic problems of his day, was scarcely touched by him. Against what he says about it in so far as he really deals with it, we have no word of criticism to offer. However, it is interesting to note that when Ninomiya came into collision with immorality at Sakuramachi, we find him appealing to religion for help to solve the problem. In so doing he did what men have always done. Little can be said about the god to which he appealed. It was a Buddhist god supposed to have power to overcome evil. Ninomiya was very anxious to succeed, and when there was a god with this reputation it was only natural that he should do as he did. The interesting thing is that the results were all that could be desired, not that the god he worshipped could possibly be accepted as satisfying the demands of a system of theism. We could not conclude that the results, obtained by an appeal to a god who was thought of as one among many gods or as one among many things, were due to anything but such influences as might operate a human experience in general. If the people believe in such a god and in the stories of his alleged influences in other cases, there would certainly be an influence of more or less importance in such an appeal. Then again, Ninomiya's appeal to the god would give him an influence with people that he might not otherwise have had. And, finally, apart from the nature of the god to whom he appealed, the earnestness of the sage and his deep anxiety for the welfare of the people would have as great an influence on them as similar facts would have at the present time. Indeed, some Japanese think that the whole incident was spectacular and that Ninomiya's intention was to work on the religious feelings and superstitions of these people rather than on the power of the god. But apart from this incident we see that Ninomiya held up this idol as an ideal for man to follow, and therefore one might conclude that he had more or less faith in its power to inspire him.

It is evident from the discussion of Ninomiya's life and teaching so far, that the question of the relation of morality and religion to economic reform is definitely before us for consideration. Ninomiya does not seem to have used morality and religion as in any sense a basis on which his economic reform might rest. He seems to introduce the moral, because without it indolent and profligate men not only could not assist in the accomplishment of his reforms, but his reforms would be a curse to them, in that more wealth would be placed at their disposal and thus hasten their destruction. On the other hand, he seems to introduce the religious more because the religious beliefs of the people were of value to him in his struggle, than because in the very nature of things it is more essential to have "a good man" than to have "a happy prosperous man." Mr. Inoue rightly describes Ninomiya as a Utilitarian, but his great object in life was not so much to develop sincerity as to save men from the misery that resulted from bad economic conditions and to make them prosperous and happy. He felt that sincerity was essential to this end.

In concluding this discussion of Ninomiya it is only necessary to point out that if we do not make morality and religion fundamental factors or needs of human nature, we cannot consistently introduce them merely as helps to effect economic reform. We cannot break man's problem into three distinct parts,— the moral, the religious, the economic. Human life is essentially a unit, of which the moral, the religious, the economic, are merely different aspects. Ninomiya came to his problem from the economic rather than from the moral or religious point of view. It is not unnatural that Japanese scholars should compare him with Christ. His unselfish devotion to human welfare is in complete accord with the spirit of Christ. To such an extent is this true that a follower of Ninomiya who really appreciates the spirit of the sage is prepared to appreciate the teachings of Jesus. But because of the prominence given to the economic, Ninomiya taught for a specific time and to meet definite conditions. His teachings are equally applicable to any time or place where similar economic conditions exist. Christ, on the other hand, made spiritual morality an end in itself. Like Ninomiya, He taught at a specific time, but He did not teach to meet conditions peculiar to His time. His problem was the moral and religious problem of man. Hence, though He was a Jew, His teaching applies equally to all human nature. He did not teach *about* the way or the moral; His presentation of truth was unique. He said, "*I* am the Way, the Truth and the Life."

SOME JAPANESE BOOKS OF REFERENCE
ON NINOMIYA IN JAPAN

"Hotoku Ki." By Mr. Tomida, Takayoshi.

"Yawa." By Mr. Fukuzumi, Masaye.

"Hotoku Ron." By Mr. Tomida, Takayoshi.

"Hotoku Gwai Ki." By Mr. Saito, Takayuki.

"Hotoku Gaku Nai Ki." By Mr. Fukuzumi, Masaye.

"Hotoku Kwan." By Mr. Fukuzumi, Masaye.

"Ninomiya wo Kenkiu." By Sapporo Agricultural School.

"Hotoku no Shinzui." By Mr. Tomeoka, Kosube.

"Ninomiya itsuwa." By Mr. Tomeoka, Kosube.

"Hotoku Issekiwa." By Mr. Tomeoka, Kosube.

"Ninomiya O to Shoka." By Mr. Tomeoka, Kosube.

"Ninomiya Sontoku to Kenmochi Hirokichi." By Mr. Tomeoka, Kosube.

"Ninomiya Sontoku to Sono Fuka." By Mr. Tomeoka, Kosube.

"Hotoku Kyo Yoryo." By Mr. Iguchi, Ushiji.

"Ninomiya Sensei Goroku." By Mr. Saito, Takayuki.

Recently a new book has been published in Japan by Tanaka Kiichi, entitled "Ninomiya Sontoku no Shin Ken Kyu," "A New Study of Ninomiya Sontoku."

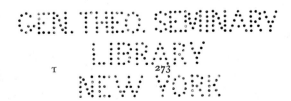

τ 273

THE following pages contain advertisements of a
few of the Macmillan books on kindred subjects

FRANK BYRON JEVONS'S

An Introduction to the History of Religion

Third Edition. Cloth, 8vo, 415 pages, $2.50 net ; by mail, $2.62

The history of early religion is here investigated on the principles and methods of anthropology; it was intended primarily for students who require an introduction to the history of religion, but has proved of interest to students of folklore, and to the wider circle of general readers. It accomplishes what no other work in the same field does, in the direction of summarizing the results of recent anthropology, estimating their bearing upon religious problems, and weaving the whole into a connected history of early religion.

HUTTON WEBSTER'S

Primitive Secret Societies

Cloth, gilt top, 8vo, $2.00 net ; by mail, $2.12

Professor Webster has grouped here, in a condensed and classified form, a great amount of information, gathered by travellers and ethnologists, on the initiation ceremonies and secret societies found among savage and barbarous communities in all parts of the world; and attempts to arrive at the significance of the facts. Particular attention is given to the almost universal, but widely varying "puberty institution" and to the part secret societies play in the tribal life and government. Magical fraternities also receive much patient attention. The prevalence and variety of mystic rites, ceremonials, and solidarities among the primitive peoples of this continent receive particular attention. The book thus becomes a storehouse of facts for the ethnological student; and it also will be of particular interest to members of the Masonic and other ancient secret orders.

PUBLISHED BY

THE MACMILLAN COMPANY
64-66 Fifth Avenue, New York

The Empire of Christ

A STUDY OF THE MISSIONARY ENTERPRISE IN
THE LIGHT OF MODERN RELIGIOUS THOUGHT

By BERNARD LUCAS

An attempt to re-state in terms which are in harmony with our altered theological thought and our changed social outlook, the old but abiding responsibility of the Church for the salvation of the world. It is an endeavor to make distinct and definite that vision of empire which was in the mind of the Church's greatest seer when he declared, "The kingdoms of this world have become the empire of our God and of His Christ."

By the author of "The Faith of a Christian," "Conversations with Christ," "The Fifth Gospel," etc.

Cloth, 12mo, $.80 net; by mail, $.89

The Religions of Eastern Asia

By HORACE GRANT UNDERWOOD, D. D.

A discussion of the various aspects of Asiatic worship—the Shintoism of Japan, and the Shamaism of Korea, in addition to the wider faiths of Taoism, Confucianism, and Buddhism. Of exceptional value to any who may come in contact with any of these forms of world-religion.

Cloth, 12mo, 267 pages, $1.50 net; by mail, $1.60

PUBLISHED BY

THE MACMILLAN COMPANY
64-66 Fifth Avenue, New York

The Second Series of Books on the

United Study of Missions

was inaugurated by the issue of

The Nearer and Farther East

COMPRISING

Moslem Lands, By the Rev. SAMUEL M. ZWEMER, D.D.
Siam, Burma, and Korea, By the Rev. ARTHUR JUDSON
BROWN, D.D.

Dr. Zwemer presents the terrible need and marvellous
opportunity of the vast, almost untouched Mohammedan fields,
while Dr. Brown paints a picture of progressive missionary
effort in comparatively small but important countries.

Outline Studies are illustrated fully with maps and refer-
ences to easily obtainable pictures, literature, etc.

"It is remarkable for the freshness of much of the information furnished." — *Baptist Teacher.*

"One of the most illuminating books for the purpose of
class study that we know." — *Christian Endeavor World.*

"The book is scholarly and accurate without, however,
losing a certain quality of literary attractiveness."
— *Christian Work and Evangelist.*

"We do not know another book so good upon lands so
little known." — *The Interior.*

Cloth, 50 cents, by mail 57 cts.; paper, 30 cents, by mail 35 cts.

PUBLISHED BY

THE MACMILLAN COMPANY

Sixty-four to Sixty-six Fifth Avenue, New York